大学英语自主听力进阶之三

LISTENING FOR SUCCESS NEWS

主编 王敏华 陈希茹

编者 沈 璟 陈希茹 邵 蕙

上海外语教育出版社
外教社 SHANGHAI FOREIGN LANGUAGE EDUCATION PRESS

图书在版编目（CIP）数据

大学英语自主听力进阶. 东西南北新闻篇 /王敏华, 陈希茹主编.
—上海：上海外语教育出版社，2008（2017重印）
ISBN 978-7-5446-0490-1

Ⅰ. 大… Ⅱ. ① 王…②陈… Ⅲ. 英语－听说教学－高等学校－教材
Ⅳ. H319.9

中国版本图书馆CIP数据核字（2007）第072799号

出版发行：上海外语教育出版社
（上海外国语大学内） 邮编：200083
电　　话：021-65425300（总机）
电子邮箱：bookinfo@sflep.com.cn
网　　址：http://www.sflep.com.cn　　http://www.sflep.com
责任编辑：杭　海

印　　刷：上海宝山译文印刷厂
开　　本：787×1092　1/16　印张 12.5　字数 312千字
版　　次：2008 年 4月第 1版　　2017 年 7月第 7次印刷
印　　数：3 500 册

书　　号：ISBN 978-7-5446-0490-1 / G・0249
定　　价：26.00 元

编者的话

关于“大学英语自主听力进阶”系列

听力理解的成功基于听者的语言知识和背景知识的相互作用。语言知识主要包括语音、词汇和句法知识等，背景知识则包括对讲话人的熟识程度、对所讲话题的熟识程度等。但有实验表明，英语学习者在听英语时主要依赖语言知识进行理解，也就是说他们的注意力集中在通过语音表达的词汇和句法结构上。这是因为听英语不同于听我们的母语，听者无暇顾及语言以外的东西。

“大学英语自主听力进阶”系列即针对这一现象专门编写，希望英语学习者在听英语时不仅关注词汇和句法结构，还要关注听力材料的背景知识和篇章结构，这样有助于更好地理解所听内容。关注篇章结构从某种意义上来说就等于注意到了句子间的联系，因而也会提高听者对所听内容的记忆强度。

“大学英语自主听力进阶”系列共分四册：《你问我答访谈篇》、《轻松睿智故事篇》、《东西南北新闻篇》和《智慧之桥讲座篇》。每册分别含有二十个单元，每个单元由Before You Listen，Listen Now，Look at This 和 Here's More 四个部分组成。各部分的主要内容和功能如下：

- Before You Listen 相当于听前热身。这部分由提问和预测 Listen Now 部分课文大意两个项目组成。在回答 Before You Listen 部分提出的问题时，听者可以激活和本单元听力内容相关的背景知识，然后浏览整个单元提供的信息（包括词汇），对 Listen Now 的大意进行预测。
- Listen Now 由两篇听力课文组成。每篇课文配有：1）词汇注释；2）对 Before You Listen 部分课文大意预测的核实练习；3）两到三项针对课文的练习。
- Look at This 针对 Listen Now 部分的听力内容提出需要注意的问题，作专门讲解。这些问题有的和读音或词句相关，有的和篇章相关，还有的则和听力内容的背景知识相关。
- Here's More 针对 Look at This 提供听力实践的机会。

以上四个部分一环扣一环，使每个单元成为一个有机的整体。而四本分册涉及日常听力活动中常见的四种体裁，难度依次递升，也使整个系列成为一个有机的整体。归纳起来，本系列图书有以下四个特点：

1、选材真实，原汁原味，既学语言，又学文化；

2、遵循认知规律，注重听前激活、听时兴趣、听后反思；

3、针对英语学习者听力理解中的普遍难点（如连词和生词等引起的听力障碍）进行精要讲解，并提供专项训练，帮助听者积累和掌握听力技能，充分体验学习和成功的喜悦；

4、听力理解与相关背景知识的掌握息息相关，因此本系列图书有针对性地介绍了和听力材料相关的背景知识。背景知识积累得越多，越有利于听力理解。

本系列的每本分册建议按如下步骤使用：

1、尝试回答每单元第一部分 Think and answer 中的提问，以激活头脑中和本单元内容有关的背景知识；

2、浏览本单元提供的信息，如词汇、练习题等，对听力材料的主要内容进行预测，以便积极主动地投入到听力实践中去；

3、听 Text One 以核实或调整预测；

4、听第二遍或第三遍，做 Text One 中其余的练习；

5、听 Text Two 以核实或调整预测；

6、听第二遍或第三遍，做 Text Two 中其余的练习；

7、阅读 Look at This；

8、做 Here's More 提供的练习。

希望英语学习者在使用"大学英语自主听力进阶"系列图书的过程中，能够感受到同一体裁听力材料的共性，从而积极主动地获取信息，这将有助于听力理解和听力记忆。我们相信，如果英语学习者能认真听完每一本分册，一定会受益匪浅，顺利通过英语专业或非专业的各类听力考试应该是意料之中的事。

关于本系列第三册《东西南北新闻篇》

新闻的种类很多，按照不同的标准有不同的分类方法。按传播工具可分为报纸新闻(newspaper coverage)、杂志新闻(magazine coverage)、广播新闻(radio news)、电视新闻(TV news)、有线电视新闻(cable news)等。按报道的内容则可分为政治新闻(political news)、经济新闻(economic news)、科技新闻(technological news)、文化新闻(cultural news)、体育新闻(sports news)、暴力与犯罪新闻(violence and crime news)、灾难新闻(disaster news)、气象新闻(weather news)和娱乐新闻(entertainment news)等。本册选材限于广播新闻和有线电视新闻，多按内容分类编排，入选的有文化新闻、体育新闻、灾难新闻、气象新闻和娱乐新闻等。每一类新闻都有其独特的一面，比如灾难新闻中必不可少的要素是灾难发生的时间、地点、伤亡人数、造成的损失等，而娱乐新闻则免不了涉及演艺界的各路明星和他们的作品。在听力实践中，如果能抓住每一类新闻的特点，将大大有利于听力理解。

编者

2007年1月

Contents

Unit 1

Childcare

Part One Before You Listen

I. Think and answer

1. Do most mothers in America stay at home to take care of their children?
2. What are the alternatives to childcare from mothers?
3. Is it easy to find good childcare in America?
4. Is childcare expensive in America? Why or why not?

II. Make your prediction

Browse through all the information offered in this unit and predict the main idea of Text One and Text Two by choosing from a, b, c and d. You may choose more than one answer to indicate your prediction.

Text One

a. Complaints of working mothers.
b. Complaints of housewives.
c. Working mothers vs. fulltime mothers.
d. Different kinds of childcare.

Text Two

a. Childcare for the poor.
b. Childcare for the rich.
c. Worries of childcare.
d. Criteria of childcare.

Part Two

Listen Now

Text One

I. Words and expressions

census /'sensəs/ *n.* 人口普查
workforce /'wɜːkfɔːs/ *n.* 劳动大军
urban /'ɜːbən/ *adj.* 城市的
nanny /'nænɪ/ *n.* 保育阿姨
au pair "互俾"姑娘，指以授课、家政服务换取膳宿的姑娘

II. Listen to confirm or to adjust

*Listen and find out if your expectations are the same as or different from what you hear. If different, find the correct one or ones from **Make your prediction**.*

III. Listen and choose the best answer to each of the following questions.

1. How many women in America with a child under six were still in the workforce according to the US Census Bureau in 2002?
   a. Sixty percent.
   b. Sixty-four percent.
   c. Thirty-four percent.
2. What's the average cost for childcare in US according to the Bureau of Labor Statistics?
   a. Four to ten thousand dollars per child per month.
   b. Four to ten thousand dollars per child per year.
   c. Four to ten thousand dollars per family per year.
3. How much did the poorest families spend on childcare in 2001 according to the Urban Institute?
   a. Half of the family income.
   b. Nine percent of the family income.
   c. Twenty-three percent of the family income.

IV. Listen and complete the following table.

Time	The way(s) childcare is given
A half century ago	1. Most mothers of young children did not work ____________.
Now	2. Sometimes ____________ or other family members watch over children. 3. Some parents employ a person to ___________ children in the parents' home. 4. Sometimes the care provider lives ____________________. 5. Au pairs are _______________ care providers. 6. Some care providers open their __________________ to one or more children. 7. Some children stay at the children's centers.

Text Two

I. Words and expressions

preschool /ˈpriːˈskuːl/ *adj.* 学前的
needy /ˈniːdɪ/ *adj.* 贫困的
hurricane /ˈhʌrɪkən/ *n.* 飓风
daycare /ˈdeɪkeə/ *adj.* 日托的
crafts /krɑːfts/ *n.* 手工艺品
federal /ˈfedərəl/ *adj.* 联邦的
median /ˈmiːdɪən/ *adj.* 中等的

II. Listen to confirm or to adjust

*Listen and find out if your expectations are the same as or different from what you hear. If different, find the correct one or ones from **Make your prediction**.*

III. Listen and decide whether the following statements are true (T) or false (F).

1. Preschool programs aim at preparing children for the educational system and life in general. *T* ☐ *F* ☐

2. Money needed to rebuild areas hit by Hurricane Katrina will surely take away from early education and childcare. *T* □ *F* □

3. Parents are mostly pleased with the price of childcare. *T* □ *F* □

4. The industry of preschool care and education has to replace many workers every year. *T* □ *F* □

5. A caregiver with a better education background usually earns more than a person who only finished high school. *T* □ *F* □

IV. Listen and fill in the following blanks.

1. The Census Bureau says there were ____________ people in poverty in 2004.
2. The poverty rate was ____________ percent, up two-tenths of one percent from the year before.
3. Currently the lowest pay in the US permitted under federal law is ____________ an hour.
4. The government says half of daycare workers earned less than ____________ ____________ an hour in 2002.
5. Those employed in schools had median earnings of ____________ per hour.

Part Three Look at This

新闻报道中的数据

新闻报道力求具有时效性、客观性、信息密集性等特点，这些特点决定了数据在新闻中的重要地位，因为数据既直接，又客观，能提供信息，又有说服力，是新闻报道不可或缺的工具。

新闻报道中的数据可分为四大类：

1. 基数：如本单元 Text One 中讲到美国人在抚养孩子方面的支出时说：

The Labor Department's Bureau of Labor Statistics says childcare costs for a full day begin at about four thousand dollars yearly. Many families pay ten thousand dollars yearly per child — and more.

2. 分数：如本单元 Text Two 中讲到美国人中穷人所占国民比例时说：

The poverty rate was twelve and seven-tenths percent, up two-tenths of one percent from the year before.

3. 百分比：如本单元 Text One 中讲到美国妇女中家有六岁以下孩童而仍旧工作的人数时说：

The United States Census Bureau said that in two thousand two, sixty-four percent of mothers with a child under age six were in the workforce.

4. 序数：比较典型地出现在体育新闻和娱乐新闻的排行榜中。

显而易见，听新闻难免会经常听到数据，在 ***Here's More*** 中我们设计了听写数据的练习。

Part Four Here's More

Exercise One

Listen twice and fill in the following blanks.

1. The I.I.E. report says the number increased by almost ________________ in the two thousand three – two thousand four school year.
2. This brought the number of Americans studying in another country to more than ______________________________________.
3. The increase the year before was ____.
4. The newest report says ___________________________ of the students went to Europe.
5. But study in China increased by __________________ percent.
6. The report says that while more Americans are studying abroad, they are staying for shorter periods of time. _________________________________ went for a full school year. ______________________ went for half a year. And ____________________ went for a shorter time.

Exercise Two

Listen twice and choose the best answer to each of the following questions.

1. What's this news report focused on?
   a. Middle schools.
   b. Elementary schools.
   c. High schools.

2. What's the news report mainly about?
   a. The improvement of schools.
   b. The increase of schools.
   c. The reduction of schools.

3. What happened in 1960?
   a. The biggest middle school opened.
   b. The first middle school opened.
   c. The last middle school opened.

4. How many middle schools is New York going to close?
   a. Up to 75.
   b. Up to 75%.
   c. None.

5. How many middle schools are there going to be in Philadelphia in 2008?
   a. 46.
   b. 48.
   c. 8.

Unit 2

Rags and Riches

Part One Before You Listen

I. Think and answer

1. Do you know anyone that migrated to other countries?
2. Do immigrants often send money back to their family in their home country? What effect does this have on the economy of their home country?
3. Do people immigrate into the more developed countries or the still developing countries? Do they often come back to work in their home countries?
4. Have you heard of General Motors? What does it produce?
5. What do businesses resort to if they are not doing well in sales?

II. Make your prediction

Browse through all the information offered in this unit and predict the main idea of Text One and Text Two by choosing from a, b, c and d. You may choose more than one answer to indicate your prediction.

Text One

a. International migration helps reduce poverty in developing countries.
b. International migration is strictly forbidden in developed countries.
c. International migration has a long history in developing countries.
d. International migration contributes to brain drain in developing countries.

Text Two

a. General Motors harvests unprecedented gains in business.
b. General Motors declares bankruptcy due to heavy losses.
c. General Motors is about to open another branch in Japan.
d. General Motors is about to cut employees to increase its competitiveness.

Part Two Listen Now

Text One

I. Words and expressions

migrant /ˈmaɪgrənt/ *n.* 移民 *adj.* 移民的
remittance /rɪˈmɪtəns/ *n.* 汇款
poverty /ˈpɒvətɪ/ *n.* 贫穷
foreign exchange 外汇
brain drain 人才流失
Guatemala /ˌgwætəˈmɑːlə/ 危地马拉(拉丁美洲国家)
Philippines /ˈfɪlɪpiːnz/ 菲律宾(东南亚岛国)
Caribbean /ˌkærɪˈbiːən/ 加勒比海

II. Listen to confirm or to adjust

Listen and find out if your expectations are the same as or different from what you hear. If different, find the correct one or ones from ***Make your prediction****.*

III. Listen and fill in the following blanks.

Some findings in the news report:

1. Families with migrant workers in other countries have ____________________ than those without migrants.
2. The migrants' remittances reduce poverty and ____________________ on education, health and investment.
3. ____________________ people are migrants living outside their native country.
4. About ______________________________ dollars will be paid in remittances this year. In many countries, remittances supply more foreign exchange than anything else.
5. The study also found that migrant workers are more likely to move to a rich nation ______________________________.
6. But international migration also means the problem of "________________."

IV. Listen and explain in what way the findings in the above exercise are convincing by choosing the best answer from the three choices to complete each of the following statements.

1. The source of all those information is a new ______________________ study.
   a. World Bank
   b. VOA
   c. UN

2. The people who conducted the study are ____________ like Maurice Schiff.
   a. journalists
   b. educationists
   c. economists

3. The findings are based on information from families in ______________ countries.
   a. three
   b. two hundred
   c. two hundred and twenty-five

Text Two

I. Words and expressions

cut /kʌt/ *n.* 裁员
bankruptcy /ˈbæŋkrəptsɪ/ *n.* 破产
automaker /ˈɔːtəʊˌmeɪkə/ *n.* 汽车制造商
competitor /kəmˈpetɪtə/ *n.* 竞争者
enforce /ɪnˈfɔːs/ *v.* 实施
chief executive officer 首席执行官

II. Listen to confirm or to adjust

*Listen and find out if your expectations are the same as or different from what you hear. If different, find the correct one or ones from **Make your prediction**.*

III. Listen and answer the following questions.

1. Who?

   ______________________.

2. Did what?

________________ a three-year plan to ____________________.

3. When?

________________________.

4. How?

a) The plan calls for GM to ____________________________ its number of workers in ______________________ by ______________________.

b) The company says it will ______________ all or part of ___________ factories in US and Canada.

IV. Listen and tick the statements that state the reasons leading GM to take those measures mentioned in the above exercise.

a. The cuts are necessary for the company to compete. ( )
b. GM has learned the maneuvers from its competitors. ( )
c. GM has lost over four thousand million dollars this year. ( )
d. GM's largest supplier, Delphi, went bankrupt this October after heavy losses. ( )
e. GM is the largest automobile maker in the world. ( )
f. GM has struggled against foreign competitors like Honda and Toyota. ( )
g. The market share for GM in US has dwindled dramatically. ( )
h. GM decides to reduce production to better meet demand. ( )

Look at This

分清新闻的来源(source)和当事人(agent)

对很多英语学习者而言，新闻难懂还有一个很实际的原因，即信息量大，涉及的因素和方面比较多，特别是当一则新闻中似乎提到不同的几个人或组织时，听众会由于弄不清其中的关系而陷入一头雾水的状态，继而因小失大，抓不住新闻报道的主要事件。

容易引起混乱的关系主要是新闻的来源(source)和当事人(agent)。当事人指的是事件的发动者(who)，对应的是who did what to whom，如本单元中Text Two讲的是通用汽车(GM)在北美裁员的打算，GM就是当事人，是事件的发动者。来源是指消息的来源，即according to whom，通常新闻为了增加报道的客观性，会提到消息的来源，如本单元中Text One讲的是移民对输出国经济的影响，为了增加可信性，也为了保持客观性，在文章的开头和当中几处提到消息的来源是世界银行（World Bank）。

由于事件的当事人和来源都可以出现在开头，而且有时在叙述上也极易混淆，所以常常让听者感到迷惑，我们的应对之策是：

1. 集中注意力于事件本身，因为抓住了事件，就很容易断定哪个是当事人，哪个是消息来源。

2. 平时留意积累有关组织的名称，这也有利于我们作出正确的判断。

3. 听时保持平和心态，如果在一开头感觉关系错综复杂，不要慌张，继续听下去，抓住关键词，听懂事件本身是最重要的，切忌因小失大。

Part Four Here's More

Exercise One

Listen twice and choose the right answer(s) to each of the following questions.

1. What's the major event in the news?
   a. An international group was named Measles Initiative.
   b. Cases of measles in Africa have decreased.

2. What does the Measles Initiative say?
   a. Cases of measles in Africa have dropped by sixty percent since 1999.
   b. Almost two hundred million children have been vaccinated against the disease in the past six years.

3. What can we learn from the World Health Organization?
   a. Many children in Africa have been saved by vaccination.
   b. Vaccination campaigns are yet to be launched in more than forty countries in Africa.

Exercise Two

Listen twice and decide whether the following statements are true (T) or false (F).

1. The news is mainly about a report published by the World Future Society. *T* ☐ *F* ☐
2. The news is provided by the World Future Society. *T* ☐ *F* ☐

3. The special report is about trends that shape the future. *T* ☐ *F* ☐

Exercise Three

Listen and choose the best answer to each of the following questions.

1. What message is conveyed in the news you have heard?
   a. Compared with 80 years ago, the number of scientists in US who believe in God has greatly dropped.
   b. About 40% of scientists in US no longer believe in God.
   c. There are about 80% of scientists in US who don't believe in God.
   d. There are roughly the same proportion of today's scientists in US believing in God as 80 years ago.

2. Which of the following statements is NOT correct according to the news you have heard?
   a. In 1916, 60% of scientists in US didn't believe in God.
   b. The University of Georgia predicted the number of scientists believing in God would be reduced with widespread education.
   c. The results of the recent survey are opposite to what has been predicted.
   d. The questions used in the recent survey are exactly the same as those in the one carried out in 1916.

Unit 3

Health

Part One Before You Listen

I. Think and answer

1. How can you maintain your health and vitality?
2. What harm do you think the quick pace of life today does to our health?
3. Do you have any bad habits that endanger your health?
4. What do you think of the current phenomenon of losing weight among young ladies?

II. Make your prediction

Browse through all the information offered in this unit and predict the main idea of Text One and Text Two by choosing from a, b, c and d. You may choose more than one answer to indicate your prediction.

Text One

a. Fascination of Chinese acupuncture.
b. How Chinese acupuncture fights against pain and other conditions.
c. Progress in Chinese acupuncture.
d. Application of Chinese acupuncture.

Text Two

a. Varieties of tea.
b. Tea and cancer.
c. Tea may help fight infection.
d. Drinking more tea.

Part Two Listen Now

Text One

I. Words and expressions

acupuncture /'ækjʊˌpʌŋktʃə/ *n.* 针灸；针刺疗法
disorder /dɪs'ɔːdə/ *n.* (身体、精神的)失调，紊乱；不适
intestine /ɪn'testɪn/ *n.* 肠
magnetic /mæg'netɪk/ *adj.* 磁的
resonance /'rezənəns/ *n.* 回声，回响；共鸣，共振
ease /iːz/ *v.* 减轻，舒缓；缓和，改善
forebrain /'fɔːbreɪn/ *n.* 前脑
cerebellum /ˌserɪ'beləm/ *n.* 小脑
brainstem /'breɪnˌstem/ *n.* 脑干
chemical /'kemɪkəl/ *n.* 化学品
dopamine /'dəʊpəmiːn/ *n.* (生化)多巴胺
endorphin /en'dɔːfɪn/ *n.* (生化)内啡肽

II. Listen to confirm or to adjust

*Listen and find out if your expectations are the same as or different from what you hear. If different, find the correct one or ones from **Make your prediction**.*

III. Listen and decide whether the following statements are true (T) or false (F).

1. American researchers have reported progress in the application of Chinese method of acupuncture. *T* ☐ *F* ☐
2. Acupuncture may help people fight against their dependence on illegal drugs according to the findings. *T* ☐ *F* ☐
3. The acupuncture study includes healthy people as well as unhealthy people. *T* ☐ *F* ☐

4. During acupuncture, if the needles are placed correctly, there will be an increase in blood in some areas of the brain. *T* ☐ *F* ☐

5. Acupuncture can ease the work of the brain. *T* ☐ *F* ☐

IV. Listen and fill in the following blanks.

1. During acupuncture, ______________________________ are placed in the skin at ______________________ on the body.
2. The study findings on acupuncture could show how ________________ might help people suffering from a number of health problems such as ________, ____________________ and ________ and some ___________ of the stomach and intestines.
3. Magnetic resonance imaging devices (MRI's) can show changes in the ________________ and the ____________________ in the blood.
4. Acupuncture reduces blood flow, which affects some brain areas and leads to _____________________, thus reducing ________________________ and helping ______________________________.

Text Two

I. Words and expressions

oolong /ˈuːlɒŋ/ *n.* 乌龙茶

pekoe /ˈpiːkəʊ/ *n.* 白毫(一种高级红茶)

antigen /ˈæntɪdʒən/ *n.* 抗原(使身体内产生抗体的物质)

interferon /ˌɪntəˈfɪərɒn/ *n.* (抗病毒等的)干扰素

arthritis /ɑːˈθraɪtɪs/ *n.* 关节炎

amino /əˈmiːnəʊ/ acid 氨基酸

II. Listen to confirm or to adjust

Listen and find out if your expectations are the same as or different from what you hear. If different, find the correct one or ones from ***Make your prediction****.*

III. Listen and define the following words and expressions.

1. L-theanine: ______
2. gamma delta T cells: ______
3. antigens: ______
4. interferon: ______
5. instant coffee: ______

IV. Listen and answer the following questions.

1. What's American researchers' opinion about drinking tea?

______

2. What did researchers do with antigens first?

______

3. How many people were tested in the study?

______

4. What do you know about the tea drinkers and the coffee drinkers as far as interferon is concerned?

______

5. What other diseases can tea help prevent according to earlier research?

______

Part Three Look at This

关注新闻报道中对专业词汇的解释

本单元的两篇新闻都是和健康有关的，免不了出现一些专业词汇。对于大多数专业词汇，我们通常会感到生疏，而在听的时候碰到生疏的词或多或少会影响听力理解。其实，大多数新闻报道似乎注意到了这一点，所以只要你留心一下，就会发现不少专业词汇后面紧跟着对这个单词或词组的解释。如第一篇新闻中提到了endorphins，下文紧接着就对这个生僻的词作了解释：These brain chemicals reduce pain and help fight feelings of sadness。从指示代词these我们可以判断brain chemicals

就是 endorphins，它们的所指相同，即大脑中产生的化学物质。又如在第二篇新闻中，我们听到了 Within twenty-four hours, the cells produced a lot of interferon, interferon 是一个专业术语，下文中提到的 a substance that fights infection 就是对它的解释。所以当我们听到某些不熟悉的专业词汇时，不妨关注接下来的信息，你可能从中找到对这些词汇的解释。另外，有些标志性的词或词组值得我们关注，如 it (this) means/refers to，that is，in other words 等，它们提醒我们这是在对前面提到的那个词或词组进行解释。定语从句有时也起词义解释作用。

Here's More

Exercise

You are going to hear ten statements and fill in the blanks.

1. Sometimes people have the idea that all cholesterol in the blood is bad. But the body needs this ________________ to create __________ and __________. The __________ produces all the cholesterol we need.

2. US health officials say there is a new epidemic; it's called obesity. As diets ______________________ become more widely available around the globe, ________________ is not just a US problem.

3. One third of all the people in the world are infected with tuberculosis, or TB, a discasc caused by ______________________. Each year, eight million infected people become sick with the disease.

4. Very different viruses that spread through ______________ or ____________________ cause hepatitis. There are five forms of hepatitis, a vital disease that ______________________.

5. People who travel on long trips should know about a condition that can develop deep inside the legs. This condition is called deep vein thrombosis. A thrombosis is ________________, a condition where some blood ______________________________.

6. Nicotine is the major substance in cigarettes that ______________________. Nicotine is ______________. The American Cancer Society says nicotine can kill a person when

______________________________.

7. Today, we tell about some ______________________________ known commonly as first aid. First aid is the kind of ________________________ given to a victim of an accident or sudden sickness before trained medical help can arrive.
8. Alcohol affects the body's reaction to the hormone insulin. Insulin helps ____________ ____________________. And alcohol may improve how the body processes blood sugar.
9. There are ________ that doctors use to ________________________. But in developing countries, not many people are able to get these antidepressants.
10. A new study warns older people against taking growth hormone supplements to reverse the effects of aging. Human growth hormone is ____________________________ important for ___________________ and ____________ of tissues and organs.

Unit 4

Sharks

Part One Before You Listen

I. Think and answer

1. What animals do you know are the oldest on Earth?
2. What do you think of sharks?
3. Have you watched any movie or read any book about sharks? If so, could you tell about it?

II. Make your prediction

Browse through all the information offered in this unit and predict the main idea of Text One and Text Two by choosing from a, b, c and d. You may choose more than one answer to indicate your prediction.

Text One

a. Sharks — one of the oldest species on Earth.
b. A brief introduction of sharks.
c. Sharks' good senses.
d. Sharks' reproduction.

Text Two

a. The importance of sharks to humans.
b. The importance of sharks to the world's oceans.
c. People's fear of sharks.
d. A book about a great white shark.

Part Two

Listen Now

Text One

I. Words and expressions

skeleton /ˈskelɪtən/ *n.* 骨骼
cartilage /ˈkɑːtɪlɪdʒ/ *n.* 软骨
reproduce /ˌriːprəˈdjuːs/ *v.* 繁殖
cord /kɔːd/ *n.* 带
fetus /ˈfiːtəs/ *n.* 胎；胎儿
dogfish shark 狗鲨
whale shark 鲸鲨
tiger shark 鼬鲨

II. Listen to confirm or to adjust

*Listen and find out if your expectations are the same as or different from what you hear. If different, find the correct one or ones from **Make your prediction**.*

III. Listen and choose the best answer to complete each of the following statements.

1. The news provided some information about ________.
   a. the existence of sharks
   b. the different kinds of sharks
   c. the length and the body structure of sharks
   d. All of the above.

2. Sharks' good senses finally help them ________.
   a. smell other sea creatures
   b. get some special power
   c. find their food
   d. kill their enemies

3. Sharks reproduce late because ________.
   a. most of them can't reproduce until they are 20 years old
   b. they reproduce every two years
   c. they can't give birth to many young sharks
   d. they grow slowly

4. About ________ of the different sharks give birth to live young, just like humans.
   a. 40%
   b. 60%
   c. 14%
   d. 86%

IV. Listen and fill in the following blanks.

1. Sharks are one of the oldest animals on Earth. They existed even before ___________ and haven't changed their way of life since ____ years ago. Now there are ___________________________________ different kinds of sharks living in the ocean. Most of them are about two meters long. But the dogfish shark is usually ____________________________ in length and ________________________ _________ can be 20 meters long. What is more interesting is sharks do not have ____________ and their skeleton is made of ____________.
2. With an excellent ___________________, a shark can find small amounts of substances in the water, such as _____________________, body liquids and _____________ produced by animals. In addition, sharks can sense _______________________ power linked to ______________________ of living animals.
3. Usually, sharks' food includes fish, other sharks, and _____________________. However, some sharks eat __________________ like shoes, dogs, a cow's foot and __________ ______________________.

Text Two

I. Words and expressions

infection /ɪn'fekʃən/ *n.* 传染病
freshwater /'freʃ'wɔːtə/ *adj.* 淡水的
aggressive /ə'gresɪv/ *adj.* 侵略性的

fierce /fɪəs/ *adj.* 凶猛的，凶狠的
coastal /ˈkəʊstəl/ *adj.* 海滨的；沿海的
version /ˈvɜːʃən/ *n.* 版本；译本；改编形式
release /rɪˈliːs/ *v.* 公开发行
Florida /ˈflɔːrɪdə/ 佛罗里达州（美国）
Nicaragua /ˌnɪkəˈræɡjʊə/ 尼加拉瓜（拉丁美洲国家）
Zambezi /zæmˈbiːzɪ/ River 赞比西河（非洲）
Mississippi /ˌmɪsɪˈsɪpɪ/ River 密西西比河（美国）
Lake Nicaragua 尼加拉瓜湖

II. Listen to confirm or to adjust

*Listen and find out if your expectations are the same as or different from what you hear. If different, find the correct one or ones from **Make your prediction**.*

III. Listen and answer the following questions.

1. Why is the study of sharks important to humans?

   ____

2. What do sharks do to protect the world's oceans?

   ____

3. What do people fear about sharks?

   ____

4. Where did the story in *Jaws* happen?

   ____

IV. Listen and decide whether the following statements are true (T) or false (F).

1. Sharks recover quickly from injuries because of their strong body defense system. *T* ☐ *F* ☐
2. With no doubt, scientists believe that shark cartilage can help humans prevent cancer and other diseases such as some infections and heart diseases. *T* ☐ *F* ☐
3. Sharks can be seen not only in the ocean but also in freshwater rivers and lakes. For example, people can find bull sharks in the Zambezi River in Africa, the Mississippi River in the United States, and Lake Nicaragua in southwestern Nicaragua. *T* ☐ *F* ☐

4. *Jaws*, originally a popular but frightening movie, told a story about how people killed a great white shark that had attacked many swimmers. *T* ☐ *F* ☐
5. Last year sixty-one people were attacked by sharks around the world and twelve of the attacks happened in waters near Florida. *T* ☐ *F* ☐

Look at This

分辨转变话题的句子　理出头绪　增强听力记忆

本单元Text One向我们介绍了鲨鱼，sharks一词从头至尾不停地灌入我们的耳朵。也许我们在听的时候感觉全部听懂了，但听完后却记不得到底听到了些什么。这种情况时常会发生在英语学习者身上。其实，这篇介绍性的文章是按顺序来向我们介绍鲨鱼的方方面面的，如果我们再仔细地听一遍Text One，就不难发现，它首先谈了鲨鱼这一物种历史悠久，几亿年前就有了，接下来谈了鲨鱼的种类等。如果我们一面听，一面把这样的头绪理出来，听过之后就不可能什么也不记得。那么怎样去理这个头绪呢？关键是要抓住转变话题的那些句子，以Text One为例，请看下面的句子：

1. Scientists say sharks have lived in the world's oceans for millions of years.
2. Scientists say there are more than three hundred fifty different kinds of sharks.
3. Sharks do not have bones.
4. A shark has an extremely good sense of smell.

以上句子的特点是shark(s)在每句句子里都是主要话题，但这四句话涉及鲨鱼的不同方面，引出了鲨鱼四个方面的情况。所以在类似的文章中，被介绍的东西是焦点，这是不言而喻的，但我们更要关注的是：话题是否转换了？涉及哪几个方面？这是一种积极主动的听力方法，它的效果比被动的、毫无目的的听要好。

在***Here's More***里，我们选了一篇介绍tundra(冻土带)的文章让大家进行这方面的练习。

Part Four Here's More

Exercise

I. Listen and rearrange the order of the following topics by writing a number from 1 to 5 beside each of them. The first one has been done for you.

Plants growing in the tundra ( )
Location and feature of the land in the tundra (1)
Animals living in the tundra ( )
Summer in the tundra ( )
Winter in the tundra ( )

II. Listen and tick the sentences which indicate changes of topics in the passage.

1. They stay as ponds, lakes and marshes during the summer. ( )
2. Tundras have very severe winters which last for about nine months of the year. ( )
3. There is some snow in the tundra, but the wind sweeps the snow away from the ground in many places. ( )
4. Summer in the tundra lasts from May to July. ( )
5. In June the tundra is blanketed with gorgeous, blooming flowers. ( )
6. About 900 different kinds of plants grow in the tundra. ( )
7. In the summer, the tundra is very busy with animal life. ( )
8. Many animals live in the tundra. ( )

Unit 5

History of Jazz

Part One Before You Listen

I. Think and answer

1. How do you like music?
2. There are many different kinds of music around us. Can you name some of them?
3. In your opinion, what kind of music is the most popular in China?
4. Have you heard of jazz? If so, would you mind sharing what you know with your classmates?

II. Make your prediction

Browse through all the information offered in this unit and predict the main idea of Text One and Text Two by choosing from a, b, c and d. You may choose more than one answer to indicate your prediction.

Text One

a. The people who introduced jazz in the program.
b. How Jazz came into being.
c. Different kinds of Jazz.
d. Some great jazz performers.

Text Two

a. Armstrong — a famous jazz musician.
b. The later development of Jazz.
c. A once-popular jazz form — swing — and some great musicians of it.
d. Another jazz form — bebop.

Part Two Listen Now

Text One

I. Words and expressions

filmmaker /ˈfɪlmˌmeɪkə/ *n.* 电影制作人
jazz /dʒæz/ *n.* 爵士乐
slavery /ˈsleɪvərɪ/ *n.* 奴隶身份；奴役
swing /swɪŋ/ *n.* 强节奏爵士乐
bebop /ˈbiːbɒp/ *n.* 博普爵士乐（盛行于20世纪40年代末到50年代初）
fusion /ˈfjuːʒən/ *n.*（不同形式音乐的）融合
note /nəʊt/ *n.* 音符
rhythm /ˈrɪðəm/ *n.* 节奏，韵律
intensity /ɪnˈtensətɪ/ *n.* 强烈，剧烈；强度，亮度
ragtime /ˈrægtaɪm/ *n.* 雷格泰姆音乐（一种早期爵士乐）
parade /pəˈreɪd/ *n.*（庆祝）游行
blues music 布鲁斯音乐
gospel /ˈgɒspəl/ music 福音音乐
New Orleans /ˈɔːlɪənz/ 新奥尔良（美国港口城市）
Louisiana /luːˌiːzɪˈænə/ 路易斯安那州（美国）

II. Listen to confirm or to adjust

*Listen and find out if your expectations are the same as or different from what you hear. If different, find the correct one or ones from **Make your prediction**.*

III. Listen and choose the best answer to each question you hear.

1. a. By radio.
   b. By TV.

c. By VOA.
d. Both *a* and *b*.

2. a. Swing.
b. Bebop.
c. Fusion of swing and bebop.
d. All of the above.

3. a. By adding new notes to music.
b. By breaking up traditional rhythms.
c. By emphasizing expected parts of music.
d. By playing a fresh and new piece.

4. a. Scott Joplin.
b. Joshua Rifkin.
c. Jelly Roll Morton.
d. King Oliver.

5. a. Jelly Roll Morton's Creole Jazz Band.
b. King Oliver's Creole Jazz Band.
c. Joshua Rifkin's Jazz Band.
d. Sidney Bechet's Jazz Band.

IV. Listen and complete the following table.

The History of Jazz (I)	
The roots of jazz	• It can be dated back to the nineteenth century. • It was generally influenced by two kinds of black music: — (1) ______________ which was created in late 1880's from gospel music and (2) ______________ of African slaves in America; — ragtime which began to be popular in (3) ______________ in the South.
The first true jazz (usually called (4) ______________ or Dixieland jazz)	• It was likely developed by African-American and Creole musicians in New Orleans in (5) ______________. • Those musicians used to (6) ______________ in memorial and holiday parades and combine their own music with (7) ______________. • Since then, they have (8) ______________ jazz to other parts of the country.

Text Two

I. Words and expressions

trumpet /ˈtrʌmpɪt/ *n.* (乐器)小号
cornet /ˈkɔːnɪt/ *n.* (乐器)短号
solo /ˈsəʊləʊ/ *n.* 独奏；独唱
orchestra /ˈɔːkɪstrə/ *n.* 管弦乐队
critic /ˈkrɪtɪk/ *n.* 评论家
clarinet /ˌklærɪˈnet/ *n.* 单簧管，黑管
symphony /ˈsɪmfənɪ/ *n.* 交响乐
solitude /ˈsɒlɪtjuːd/ *n.* 孤独
Chicago /ʃɪˈkɑːgəʊ/ 芝加哥(美国城市)

II. Listen to confirm or to adjust

*Listen and find out if your expectations are the same as or different from what you hear. If different, find the correct one or ones from **Make your prediction**.*

III. Listen and decide whether the following statements are true (T) or false (F).

1. In addition to his unusual voice, Louis Armstrong was also famous for the performance on the trumpet and on the jazz cornet. *T* ☐ *F* ☐
2. The young people from the Middle West of America created Chicago-style jazz. *T* ☐ *F* ☐
3. Swing music got its name from a song by Duke Ellington — "Sing, Sing, Sing (with a Swing)." *T* ☐ *F* ☐
4. "Symphony" was a new musical form before World War II. *T* ☐ *F* ☐
5. Critics praised everything about Goodman except his playing of the clarinet. *T* ☐ *F* ☐
6. Billie Holiday used to perform with some big bands and one of the most famous song of his is "Solitude." *T* ☐ *F* ☐

IV. Listen and complete the following table.

The History of Jazz (II)	
1920's: the Jazz Age (or (1) ______________ ______ of American Jazz)	● During the age, a new musical form — Chicago-style jazz — was created. ● During this time, a number of (2) ____________________ came forth such as Gene Krupa and Benny Goodman.
The development of jazz until after World War II	● A new jazz form — swing — became very popular in America. ● During this period, many jazz musicians made great contribution. Goodman was the best-known among them. — He was called (3) "____________________." — He was the first jazz clarinetist to (4) ______________ _______. — With his help, (5) ____________________ jazz musicians played together for the first time. — He (6) ________________ great African-American jazz artists.
The development of jazz after World War II	● Bebop replaced swing as the most popular jazz.

Part Three Look at This

抓住年代　理出顺序　有助听力理解

本单元的新闻报道介绍了爵士乐的起源、发展和影响。不知你听的时候是否注意到它是按年代顺序来讲述的——从19世纪起一直到第二次世界大战后，每个年代都有不同的爵士乐流派、代表人物和音乐作品。所以我们听类似的新闻报道时，应该关注什么年代发生了什么，抓住了这些东西，就抓住了全文的要点。在 ***Here's More*** 里我们选了一篇介绍奥运会历史的文章供大家进行这方面的练习。

另外，本单元介绍的是爵士乐的历史，如果对音乐方面的知识有所了解，听起来会更得心应手一些。为此，我们选编了一些音乐词汇，并且在 ***Here's More*** 中选入了谈论各种不同音乐的短文，希望帮助大家积累这方面的知识。

有关音乐的一些词汇

1. 不同的音乐类型

classic(al) music（古典音乐），blues（布鲁斯/蓝调），folk（民谣），pop（流行乐），jazz（爵士乐），rock（摇滚乐），country（乡村音乐），hip hop（嘻哈乐），dance（舞曲），rap（说唱），blue-eyed soul（灵魂乐），Celtic（凯尔特音乐），New Age（新浪潮音乐），computer music（计算机音乐），electronica（电子音乐），world（世界音乐），surf（海浪音乐）

当然以上这些音乐还可以进一步细分，以摇滚乐为例，又可以分为soft rock（慢摇滚），hard rock/heavy metal（硬摇滚/重金属摇滚），rap-rock（说唱摇滚），pub rock（酒吧摇滚），post-rock（后摇滚），Latin rock（拉丁摇滚），jazz-rock（爵士摇滚），folk-rock（民谣摇滚），grunge（垃圾摇滚），Celtic rock（凯尔特摇滚），arena rock（舞台摇滚），American trad rock（美国传统摇滚），alternative rock（另类摇滚），acid rock（酸性摇滚）等。

2. 乐曲特征及相关词汇

tempo（速度），range（音域），time（拍子），bar（小节），rhythm（节奏），tone（音色），pitch（音高），major key（大调），minor key（小调），introduction（前奏），melody（主旋律），chorus（副歌），lyrics/words（歌词），score（总谱），octave（八度音阶）

3. 乐器及相关词汇

violin（小提琴），viola（中提琴），cello（大提琴），double bass（低音提琴或大贝司），flute（长笛），piccolo（短笛），clarinet（单簧管），oboe（双簧管），bassoon（大管），trumpet（小号），cornet（短号），tuba（大号），harp（竖琴），organ（风琴），xylophone（木琴），mandolin（曼陀林），guitar（吉他），the winds（管乐器），the strings（弦乐器），keyboard（键盘），sound box（共鸣箱），mouthpiece（吹口），reed（簧片），piston（活塞阀键），valve（改变音调的活瓣），pipe（风管），pedal（踏板），hammer（音锤）

Part Four Here's More

Exercise One

I. Listen and write down the times you hear. The first one has been done for you.

1. more than 2,700 years ago
2. ______________________
3. ______________________
4. ______________________
5. ______________________

II. Listen and write down what happened in the different times you have written in the above exercise. The first one has been done for you.

1. More than 2,700 years ago, the Olympics began.
2. ______________________________
3. ______________________________
4. ______________________________
5. ______________________________

Exercise Two

You will hear what a young music fan considers as different types of music. Listen and number the types of music in the order you hear them in the recording.

( ) hip hop
( ) dance music
( ) rock & roll
( ) classical
( ) folk
( ) blues

Unit 6

Thanksgiving Holiday

Part One Before You Listen

I. Think and answer

1. Where is Thanksgiving Day celebrated?
2. According to its name, can you guess the meaning of this holiday?
3. Do you know how people celebrate Thanksgiving Day? (e.g. activities and food)
4. Do you have a similar holiday in your country? If so, what is it?

II. Make your prediction

Browse through all the information offered in this unit and predict the main idea of Text One and Text Two by choosing from a, b, c and d. You may choose more than one answer to indicate your prediction.

Text One

a. A brief introduction of Thanksgiving Day.
b. A purely American holiday — Thanksgiving Day.
c. Some typical examples of people from different backgrounds celebrating Thanksgiving Day.
d. A writer's understanding of Thanksgiving Day.

Text Two

a. People's worries about bird flu.
b. A family keeps the tradition of observing the holiday for many years.
c. What people eat and do on Thanksgiving Day.
d. A lot of people don't celebrate the holiday.

Part Two Listen Now

Text One

I. Words and expressions

harvest /ˈhɑːvɪst/ *v.* 收割
spiritual /ˈspɪrɪtjʊəl/ *adj.* 精神上的，心灵的
reunion /ˌriːˈjuːnjən/ *n.* 团聚
Muslim /ˈmʊzlɪm/ *adj.* 伊斯兰教的； *n.* 伊斯兰教信徒
observance /əbˈzɜːvəns/ *n.* 遵守，奉行；仪式
Ramadan /ˌræməˈdæn/ *n.* 斋月（该月内伊斯兰教徒白天禁食）
Thanksgiving Day 感恩节
corn pudding 玉米布丁（一种食物）
New Jersey /ˈdʒɜːzɪ/ 新泽西州（美国）
Maryland /ˈmeərɪlænd/ 马里兰州（美国）

II. Listen to confirm or to adjust

Listen and find out if your expectations are the same as or different from what you hear. If different, find the correct one or ones from ***Make your prediction****.*

III. Listen and answer the following questions.

1. When is Thanksgiving Day celebrated?

   ____

2. What did O. Henry think of Thanksgiving Day?

   ____

3. What activity is the main celebration on that day?

   ____

4. How many people usually come to Ms. Scott-Buczak's home and have dinner on that day?

   ____

5. What is Eid al-Fitr?

____

6. How many countries did Subhash Vohra work in as a journalist before he came to the US?

____

IV. Listen and decide whether the following statements are true (T) or false (F).

1. For many people in the US, Thanksgiving Day is the only time of their family reunion. *T* ☐ *F* ☐
2. Ms. Scott-Buczak prepares a big dinner for Thanksgiving Day every year and invites her relatives as well as all their friends. *T* ☐ *F* ☐
3. In Ms. Scott-Buczak's home, children and adults usually sit at the same table and enjoy the big dinner together. *T* ☐ *F* ☐
4. According to the news, sweet potato pie and corn pudding are quite popular among some African Americans. *T* ☐ *F* ☐
5. Ismaila Sanghua loves to celebrate Thanksgiving Day much more than his children do. *T* ☐ *F* ☐
6. Although born in India, Subhash Vohra — the VOA producer, writer and editor — has celebrated Thanksgiving Day together with his wife and two sons for many years since he came to the US. *T* ☐ *F* ☐
7. "Give Good Gifts One to Another" is an old American song especially for Thanksgiving. *T* ☐ *F* ☐

Text Two

I. Words and expressions

poultry /ˈpəʊltrɪ/ *n.* (总称)家禽
infect /ɪnˈfekt/ *v.* 传染
deadly /ˈdedlɪ/ *adj.* 致命的
cranberry /ˈkrænbərɪ/ *n.* 越橘
pumpkin /ˈpʌmpkɪn/ *n.* 南瓜
vegetarian /ˌvedʒɪˈteərɪən/ *n.* 素食者
avian /ˈeɪvɪən/ *adj.* 鸟的，鸟类的
influenza /ˌɪnfluˈenzə/ *n.* 流行性感冒

bird flu/avian influenza 禽流感
Virginia /və'dʒɪnjə/ 弗吉尼亚州(美国)

II. Listen to confirm or to adjust

Listen and find out if your expectations are the same as or different from what you hear. If different, find the correct one or ones from ***Make your prediction****.*

III. Listen and choose the best answer to each question you hear.

1. a. More than 30 years.
   b. About 30 years.
   c. Less than 13 years.
   d. Almost 13 years.

2. a. For those who couldn't return home for the holiday.
   b. For those who were also from the Midwest.
   c. For those who had babies and young children.
   d. For the new friends they made in Virginia.

3. a. Bread.
   b. A kind of brandy mixture.
   c. A cooked bread mixture.
   d. A meal.

4. a. Turkeys imported from Europe.
   b. Turkeys infected with bird flu.
   c. All the poultry infected with avian influenza.
   d. The poultry coming from Asia.

5. a. A city.
   b. A store.
   c. A person.
   d. A parade.

IV. Listen and fill in the following blanks. (One word for each blank.)

1. Besides turkey, other traditional Thanksgiving foods include ________, a ________ fruit called cranberries and ______ pie.
2. Although turkey is the main traditional Thanksgiving dish, at a ________ dinner, no turkey or other meats will be served.
3. Now on Thanksgiving Day, people watch several professional and ________ ________ games on __________ television. The games are regarded as a _______ ________ of

Thanksgiving celebration.

4. Besides, Thanksgiving Day ________ on TV are very welcome to many Americans, which are usually ________ by big ________ in several cities.

Part Three Look at This

利用上下文和标志性的词来判断名称的属类

在各类英语新闻中，我们时常会听到各种各样的名称，有地名、人名、歌名、节日名称、商店名称、公司名称、球队名称等等。在听到一些不熟悉的英文名称时，我们往往不知所云，这影响了我们对所听文章的理解。遇到这种情况，我们可以利用上下文及一些标志性的词，积极思考并推测名称的含义。例如，本单元听力材料中有一段内容：

Many people also like to watch Thanksgiving Day parades on television. Big stores in several cities organize these parades. For example, **Macy's** has a very famous Thanksgiving Day parade in New York.

乍一听，Macy's 好像是人名，但是结合上下文来看：一些大商场组织庆祝游行，而Macy's 组织这类游行是大商场组织游行的一个例子，所以可以推断Macy's是商场名称。

还有这么一句：

Alma Scott-Buczak gathers her family for Thanksgiving dinner every year.

her 这个代词指代了前面出现的人物，所以不难判断 Alma Scott-Buczak 是一位女士的名字。

至于其他标志性的词，以对人的称呼为例，有表示称谓的词，如Mr., Mrs., Miss, Ms., Sir等；有表示职位、头衔的词，如CEO, chief, chancellor, governor, president, editor 等；这些词后出现的名称一般为人名。

一些和地方有关或表示方向的词或词组（如 area，town，city，state，island，northern，in the south of 等）可以看作引出地名的标志性词。

其他的还有：called 及前面出现的名词，如 the company called + 公司名称，the song called + 歌曲名称；for example/such as/like 及前面出现的名词，如 some popular books, for example, + 书名；include 及前面出现的名词，如 The country has other insular islands. They include + 岛屿名称；等等。

表示并列或比较关系的词或词组（如 and，as well as，together with，compared to 等）前后连接的名称往往属于同一种类。

Here's More

Exercise

You will hear some statements with different kinds of names. Listen and tell what these names refer to.

Example

You hear:

The project is led by Nicholas Negroponte, Chief of the Media Lab at the Massachusetts Institute of Technology.

The exercise:

Nicholas Negroponte: the name of Chief of the Media Lab

1. **Mitt Romney**: the name of ____________________ of Massachusetts
2. **Angela Merkel**: the name of ____________________ of Germany
3. **Zinder**: the name of ____________________
4. **Thai Thu Thu**: the name of ____________________
5. **Tikipia/Anuta/Fataka**: the name of ____________________
6. **Lavender Mist**: the name of ____________________
7. **WKYS**: the name of ____________________
8. **FC Basel**: the name of ____________________
9. **Katrina**: the name of ____________________
10. **Jay Z**: the name of ____________________
    Roca-a-Fella: the name of ____________________
11. **Starbuck O'Dwyer**: the name of ____________________
    Sky Thorne: the name of ____________________
    Tailburger: the name of ____________________
12. **Ruth Brown**: the name of ____________________
    Lucky Lips: the name of ____________________
13. **Sonia Flew**: the name of ____________________
    Melinda Lopez: the name of ____________________
    Hanukkah: the name of ____________________

Unit 7 Studying Abroad

Part One Before You Listen

I. Think and answer

1. Do you plan to pursue further study abroad after graduation from college? If so, which country do you want to go to?
2. What, in your opinion, are the different approaches to learning between Chinese and American students?
3. Name some American universities you know. Why is the US attractive to many Chinese students who want to study abroad?
4. Why do some people say that the American universities become more and more international?

II. Make your prediction

Browse through all the information offered in this unit and predict the main idea of Text One and Text Two by choosing from a, b, c and d. You may choose more than one answer to indicate your prediction.

Text One

a. More students in developing countries pursue study abroad.
b. The number of foreign students in US decreases dramatically.
c. The drop in the number of foreign students in US slows.
d. The number of Americans studying abroad continues to rise.

Text Two

a. Foreign students at US colleges have several ways to get financial aid.

b. Exchange is a cost-saving way to study at a US college.
c. American students have several ways to finance their college study.
d. American students prefer to study abroad.

Part Two Listen Now

Text One

I. Words and expressions

archive /ˈɑːkaɪv/ *n.* 搜索引擎
quotation /kwəʊˈteɪʃən/ mark 引号
Los Angeles /lɒsˈændʒələs/ 洛杉矶(美国城市)
Illinois /ˌɪlɪˈnɔɪ(z)/ 伊利诺斯州(美国)
Urbana-Champaign 乌班那－香槟分校(伊利诺斯大学的一个校区)

II. Listen to confirm or to adjust

Listen and find out if your expectations are the same as or different from what you hear. If different, find the correct one or ones from ***Make your prediction****.*

III. Listen and choose the best answer to each question you hear.

1. a. More than 80,000.
   b. More than 565,000.
   c. A little below 2,000,000.
   d. A little below 1,000,000.

2. a. China.
   b. South Korea.
   c. Japan.
   d. India.

3. a. Difficulties in getting a student visa.
   b. Higher costs.

c. Competition from the American students.

d. Competition from schools in other English-speaking countries.

IV. Listen and decide whether the following statements are true (T) or false (F).

1. The number of foreign students in American universities increased last school year compared with the year before. T ☐ F ☐
2. India has the largest increase in the number of students sent to the US last school year. T ☐ F ☐
3. Only one hundred forty-five American colleges and universities had international students last year according to the report. T ☐ F ☐
4. The number of international students decreased mainly because of three reasons according to the report. T ☐ F ☐

Text Two

I. Words and expressions

grant /grɑːnt/ *n.* (尤指国家发给的)补助金，助学金
loan /ləʊn/ *n.* 贷款
fellowship /ˈfeləʊʃɪp/ *n.* (发给大学研究生的)学术奖金
Missouri /mɪˈzʊərɪ/ 密苏里州(美国)

II. Listen to confirm or to adjust

*Listen and find out if your expectations are the same as or different from what you hear. If different, find the correct one or ones from **Make your prediction**.*

III. Listen and answer the following questions.

1. What are the four kinds of financial aid mentioned in this education report?

____

2. What does a student do if he or she wants to get an assistantship?

____

3. What's the difference between grants and loans?

____

4. What's the difference between scholarships and fellowships?

____

5. How can students get scholarships from a university?

____

IV. Listen and fill in the following blanks.

1. An assistantship is ________________________. In exchange, the student ________________________ or ________________________.
2. A grant is ____. Grants are generally given to students who need the money by ________________________ ______________.
3. Scholarships and fellowships are ______________________________ going to students with ________________________ or ______________________.
4. The University of Missouri in Columbia has two financial aid programs for international students, that is, ______________________________ and the ______________ __________________.

Part Three Look at This

留学美国

在本系列图书第一册《你问我答访谈篇》中，我们谈到过美国的大学。美国有2 000多所授予学位的四年制大学院校，另有1 800多所两年制学院和“社区大学”。这里我们要说的是赴美留学。

美国是向外国留学生提供经费资助最多的国家，同时也是招收外国留学生最多、获得经济回报最高的国家。近十多年来每年有五六十万左右国际学生在美国读书，占全球在非本国本地区高等院校就读学生总数的三到四成。尤其重要的是，在这些留学生中，攻读学士、硕士和博士学位的学生占总数的92.2%。这样多的高层次留学生人数，是目前任何其他西方发达国家可望而不可及的，而其中相当一部分学生毕业后即将充实进美国的科研机构和高等院校，为美国提供高级人才达数十万。

由美国国际教育研究所（IIE）收集的年度统计数据显示，2003–2004学年度有

61 765名中国学生在美国接受高等教育，占外国留美学生总人数的近11%。留美的中国学生中82%是研究生。在美国主修数学、自然科学和工程的中国学生，往往能够胜任助教和助理研究员工作，这样还能获得减免学费的资格。

Part four Here's More

Exercise

You are going to hear a passage twice and answer the following questions.

1. What are the characteristics of the American system of higher education?
____

2. How many universities make up the Ivy League?
____

3. What do you know about Georgetown University as far as its foundation is concerned?
____

4. What can you know about the old teacher's colleges and agricultural schools from this passage?
____

5. For how many reasons can we say that the American system of higher education is innovative?
____

6. What are the greatest rewards of their time of study in the United States according to most returned Chinese students?
____

Unit 8

Bird Flu

Part One Before You Listen

I. Think and answer

1. What is bird flu? How does it spread to humans?
2. What can you do to prevent yourself from contracting bird flu?
3. What can the government do to prevent this contagious disease from spreading from domesticated fowls to humans?
4. Can man finally defeat this disease?

II. Make your prediction

Browse through all the information offered in this unit and predict the main idea of Text One and Text Two by choosing from a, b, c and d. You may choose more than one answer to indicate your prediction.

Text One

a. Panic about bird flu prevails all over the world.
b. No need to panic in areas with no bird flu outbreak.
c. In bird flu affected areas precautionary measures should be taken.
d. Causes of bird flu remain unknown.

Text Two

a. EU's effort to prevent the spread of bird flu.
b. Outbreak of bird flu in Russia is beyond control.
c. Outbreak of bird flu in some Asian countries is beyond control.
d. Measures have been taken in various regions and countries to control the spread of bird flu.

Part Two

Listen Now

Text One

I. Words and expressions

plummet /ˈplʌmɪt/ *v.* 陡直落下；骤然下跌
outbreak /ˈaʊtbreɪk/ *n.* (坏事的)突然发生，爆发
slaughter /ˈslɔːtə/ *v.* 屠宰，宰杀
precautionary /prɪˈkɔːʃənərɪ/ *adj.* 预防的
hygienic /haɪˈdʒiːnɪk/ *adj.* 卫生的
contamination /kənˌtæmɪˈneɪʃən/ *n.* 污染
utensil /juːˈtensəl/ *n.* 器皿，用具
disinfect /ˌdɪsɪnˈfekt/ *v.* (给东西、场所)消毒(杀菌)

II. Listen to confirm or to adjust

Listen and find out if your expectations are the same as or different from what you hear. If different, find the correct one or ones from ***Make your prediction****.*

III. Listen and decide whether the following statements are true (T) or false (F).

1. Sales of chicken have plummeted because of the outburst of bird flu according to a WHO official. *T* ☐ *F* ☐
2. People are advised not to eat undercooked chicken and eggs. *T* ☐ *F* ☐
3. People should not eat diseased flocks, but infected birds can be used for animal feed. *T* ☐ *F* ☐
4. Avian flu can be prevented in affected areas by taking some precautionary measures. *T* ☐ *F* ☐

IV. Listen and answer the following questions.

1. Why is there no need to panic about eating chicken according to a WHO official?

____

2. Why should poultry meat and eggs be properly cooked before consumed?

____

3. Do people run the risk of getting the virus through handling or eating poultry where there is no bird flu outbreak?

____

4. What precautionary measures should people take when they slaughter and handle diseased or dead birds in affected areas?

____

Text Two

I. Words and expressions

veterinary /ˈvetərɪnərɪ/ *adj.* 兽医的
endorse /ɪnˈdɔːs/ *v.* 赞同，认可，支持
territory /ˈterɪtərɪ/ *n.* 地区，地方
domesticate /dəʊˈmestɪkeɪt/ *v.* 驯养（动物）
prompt /prɒmpt/ *v.* 促使，引起
quarantine /ˈkwɒrəntiːn/ *n.* 检疫，隔离 *v.* 隔离
detect /dɪˈtekt/ *v.* 发现，发觉
pathogen /ˈpæθədʒɪn/ *n.* 病原体
migratory /ˈmaɪgrətərɪ/ *adj.* 迁徙的
preliminary /prɪˈlɪmɪnərɪ/ *adj.* 初步的，预备的
contract /kənˈtrækt/ *v.* 感染（疾病）
cull /kʌl/ *v.* （从一群动物中）剔除
succumb /səˈkʌm/ *v.* 屈服，不再抗拒
trumpet /ˈtrʌmpɪt/ *v.* 大肆宣扬，鼓吹
brace /breɪs/ *v.* 准备迎接（困难），振作精神

II. Listen to confirm or to adjust

*Listen and find out if your expectations are the same as or different from what you hear. If different, find the correct one or ones from **Make your prediction**.*

III. Listen and complete the following table.

Location	1. ______________________.
Symptom	2. ______________________.
Cause of the outbreak	3. ______________________.
Measures taken by Russian authorities	4. ______________________.
Measures taken by EU	5. ______________________.

IV. Listen and fill in the following blanks.

In southeast Asia, at least (1) ________ people have contracted the bird flu virus in the past two years, resulting in at least (2) ________ deaths in (3) ______________, (4) ______________, (5) ______________ and (6) ______________. In Thailand, the 13th confirmed human death is a (7) ________-year-old farmer. In China, the epidemic situation is under control after more than (8) ________ birds were culled from a farm in (9) __________________________. Measures have been taken to (10) ________, (11) ________, or (12) ________ and (13) ________ according to regulations after the Chinese government received the report of suspected bird flu.

Part Three Look at This

新闻报道中的组织、机构和条约名称以及它们的缩略形式

世界上有各种国际性或区域性的组织和条约，每个国家也有各自的国内组织机构。一些组织、机构和条约的名称在新闻报道中出现频率较高，如本单元两则新闻中分别提到的 World Health Organization 和 EU。有时不了解这类名称，就会给整条新闻的理解带来障碍。所以，为了更好地理解英语新闻，有必要了解一下这些名称以及它们在新闻广播节目中的出现形式。

一般来说，由于各种组织、机构和条约的全称都比较长，所以它们都有自己的缩略形式，使用缩略词传递信息既简单明了，又节约时间。在新闻广播中，这类名称第一次往往会以全称的形式出现，以后再提及时用缩略形式；或者先以缩略形式出现，紧接着介绍其全称。有些很常用的名称常常只以缩略形式出现。

缩略词可分为两类，即 acronym 和 initialism。它们的不同之处在于： acronym

像普通单词一样把字母连起来拼读，如APEC，NATO等；而initialism则按字母单个拼读，如WTO，WHO等。

我们应该注意以下几点：

1. 弄清这类名称的全称和缩略形式，并注意缩略形式大都为大写字母组成。

2. 掌握它们之间不同的发音规则。

3. 理解时应特别注意，同一个acronym或initialism有时具有不同的含义，表示不同的组织、机构或条约。

下面就世界上一些知名的组织作一简单归纳：

International Court of Justice 国际法院

Security Council 安全理事会

General Assembly 联合国大会

United Nations Educational, Scientific and Cultural Organization (UNESCO) 联合国教育、科学及文化组织

World Health Organization (WHO) 世界卫生组织

World Meteorological Organization (WMO) 世界气象组织

World Trade Organization (WTO) 世界贸易组织

International Finance Corporation (IFC) 国际金融公司

International Monetary Fund (IMF) 国际货币基金组织

International Bank for Reconstruction and Development (IBRD) 世界银行

European Economic Community (EEC) 欧洲经济共同体

African Union (AU) 非洲联盟

European Union (EU) 欧洲联盟

Group of Eight Summit (G8 Summit) 八国集团首脑会议

Group of Twenty (G20) 二十国集团

International Olympic Committee (IOC) 国际奥林匹克委员会

National Aeronautics and Space Administration (NASA) 美国国家航空航天局

Federal Bureau of Investigation (FBI) 美国联邦调查局

Food and Drug Administration (FDA) 美国食品及药物管理局

Organization of Petroleum Exporting Countries (OPEC) 石油输出国组织

Asia Pacific Economic Cooperation (APEC) 亚洲及太平洋地区经济合作组织

North Atlantic Treaty Organization (NATO) 北大西洋公约组织

Association of South-East Asian Nations (ASEAN) 东南亚国家联盟

Palestine Liberation Organization (PLO) 巴勒斯坦解放组织

Part Four Here's More

Exercise

You are going to hear a passage twice and answer the following questions.

1. What's the difference between an acronym and an initialism?

   ____

2. What is the growing problem for English speakers as far as an acronym or initialism is concerned?

   ____

3. What strong desire does the American writer H. L. Mencken find that Americans have?

   ____

4. How many acronyms could be found in the English Language back in 1960 and what's the number now?

   ____

Unit 9

Economy

Part One Before You Listen

I. Think and answer

1. Can you name in English some of the economic organizations in the world?
2. What do "Asian's four little dragons" and "Asian's four little tigers" refer to?
3. What changes has China witnessed since its opening and reform?
4. What benefits will China's sound and rapid economic development bring to other Asian countries?

II. Make your prediction

Browse through all the information offered in this unit and predict the main idea of Text One and Text Two by choosing from a, b, c and d. You may choose more than one answer to indicate your prediction.

Text One

a. India and Japan's economic cooperation.
b. Problems with India and Japan's economic cooperation.
c. India and Japan seek to improve trade.
d. Advantages of India and Japan's trade cooperation.

Text Two

a. Economic cooperation between Asia and Africa.
b. Elements hampering Asia and Africa's development.
c. Problems concerning Asia's development.
d. Problems concerning Africa's development.

Part Two Listen Now

Text One

I. Words and expressions

soaring /ˈsɔːrɪŋ/ *adj.* 腾飞的，剧增的
fiscal /ˈfɪskəl/ *adj.* 财政的
symposium /sɪmˈpəʊzɪəm/ *n.* 专题研讨会，讨论会
induce /ɪnˈdjuːs/ *v.* 引起，导致
infrastructure /ˈɪnfrəˌstrʌktʃə/ *n.* 基础设施
bureaucratic /ˌbjʊərəʊˈkrætɪc/ *adj.* 官僚主义的，官僚作风的
counter /ˈkaʊntə/ *v.* 反击，对抗
comprehensive /ˌkɒmprɪˈhensɪv/ *adj.* 全面的，综合的
pact /pækt/ *n.* 协定，协议，条约
Mitsubishi /mɪˈtzʊbɪʃɪ/ （日本）三菱电机

II. Listen to confirm or to adjust

*Listen and find out if your expectations are the same as or different from what you hear. If different, find the correct one or ones from **Make your prediction**.*

III. Listen and decide whether the following statements are true (T) or false (F).

1. Japan's share of total India trade was nearly 4 percent in the 2005–2006 fiscal year. *T* ☐ *F* ☐
2. Japan has sufficient new investment in India, therefore, it's the third largest investor in India. *T* ☐ *F* ☐
3. India and Japan disagree on the reasons leading to the current level of Japanese trade in India. *T* ☐ *F* ☐

4. Japan and India have reached a comprehensive economic partnership agreement. *T* ☐ *F* ☐

IV. Listen and fill in the following blanks.

1. The two persons who spoke at the India-Japan Strategic Partnership Symposium are Rakesh Mohan, ______________________________, and Mikio Sasaki, ______________________________.
2. According to Japanese investors, Japan's current level of trade in India is caused by ____________________________, ____________________________, ______________________________ and ______________________________.
3. India's business faces ________________ for chemicals and medicines and ________________ on seafood when expanding exports to Japan.

Text Two

I. Words and expressions

globalization /ˌgləʊbəlaɪˈzeɪʃən/ *n.* 全球化
summit /ˈsʌmɪt/ *n.* 峰会，政府首脑会议
partake /pɑːˈteɪk/ *v.* 参加(活动)，参与
strategic /strəˈtiːdʒɪk/ *adj.* 战略上的；重要的，有用的
equitable /ˈekwɪtəbl/ *adj.* 公平的，公正的
institute /ˈɪnstɪtjuːt/ *n.* 协会，学院，研究院
draft /drɑːft/ *n.* 草案，草稿
specificity /ˌspesɪˈfɪsətɪ/ *n.* 特征；特殊性
operative /ˈɒpərətɪv/ *n.* 技术工
stride /straɪd/ *n.* 进展，发展，进步

II. Listen to confirm or to adjust

Listen and find out if your expectations are the same as or different from what you hear. If different, find the correct one or ones from ***Make your prediction****.*

III. Listen and complete the following table.

Time	1. Begins ______________________.
Event	2. ______________________.
Place	3. ______________________.
Participants	4. ______________________.
Purpose	5. To reach mutually beneficial ______________________ through ______________________ between ______ and ______________.

IV. Listen and choose the best answer to each question you hear.

1. a. To work more effectively together to build a more equitable world financial economic structure.
   b. To have a bigger voice in the reforms of multi-lateral institutes.
   c. To put their colonial past behind them and take their place on the world stage.
   d. To reap the benefits of globalization.

2. a. In Bandung, Indonesia.
   b. In Bombay, India.
   c. In Jakarta, Indonesia.
   d. In Lagos, Nigeria.

3. a. Because they didn't share their experience of economic development with each other.
   b. Because the globalization has little or no regard for third-world countries, and its sole purpose is to make profits at the expense of almost all else.
   c. Because they didn't cooperate well with each other.
   d. Because there is no cooperation between Asian and African private sector operatives.

Part Three Look at This

新闻报道中的人名、国名和头衔

在收听英语新闻时，人名的出现频率极高。人名主要指各国的主要领导人(包括国王、国家元首、政府首脑、外交部长、国防部长和各部门的新闻发言人等)、各大国际组织的头号人物以及一些重要的新闻人物(包括在野党首要领导、反对派领导人等)的名字。人名一般都比较长，而且有些非英语国家的人名特别难记，有的更是和汉语译名的读音“风马牛不相及”，我们听过后想记住这些名字比较困难。怎样来解决这个问题呢？

听到人名时，我们应克服自己的紧张情绪。收听新闻时能不能记住人名有时并不十分关键。如果我们了解足够数量的国名及该国首都名称，听时就比较容易搞清楚这些难记的要人姓名所代表的国家和政府；再熟记一些表示头衔的词，那么即使在听的时候记不住那些让我们头痛的人名，也不会妨碍我们准确地理解新闻内容。这是因为在新闻广播中，每当提到某要人时，其格式通常是：国籍 + 职位或身份 + 姓名，这三项中，如果我们能听懂前面两项，就能基本上把握新闻的意思。例如本单元第二则报道中提到 Indonesian President Susilo Bambang Yudhoyono 和 Nigerian President Olusegun Obasanjo，要记住这两位的名字比较难，所以知道两人分别是印度尼西亚总统和尼日利亚总统即可。不过那些经常出现在新闻当中的人名，我们必须下功夫记住它们，这会有助于我们理解英语新闻。

我们在平时的学习中还要留心注意表示国籍和常用职位的词。如果我们听不懂人名前面的国籍、职务和官衔(如chancellor指某些国家的总理或大臣，admiral指海军上将)，或把它们当作人名的一部分而不加注意，就会影响对新闻内容的理解。姓和名形形色色，千变万化，难以把握，但表示国籍和头衔的词却是我们通过努力可以掌握的。

Here's More

Exercise

You are going to hear ten news headlines and fill in the following blanks.

1. The ______________________ Donald Rumsfeld has arrived in Britain for talks with the ______________________ Tony Blair on situation in Iraq and Afghanistan.
2. The ______________________ Colin Powell is holding talks in Damascus today with the ______________________ Bashar al-Asad.
3. ______________________ Bush has given a task of creating an interregnum Iraqi government to a ______________________ Paul Bremer.
4. The ______________________ Michael Jackson is suing the Motown record label for money he says he has owned in royalties for several classic songs.
5. ______________________ George Robinson held talks with ______________________ Putin and senior government ministers.

6. The ____________________ Javie Solana has had meetings on the new Middle East peace initiative with the ____________________ Yasser Arafat and the Palestinian Prime Minister.
7. The ____________________ Ariel Sharon has met his ____________________ Mahmoud Abbas, also known as Abu Mazen, in Jerusalem for the first time to discuss the American-backed peace plan, known as the Road Map.
8. A ____________________ Andrew Mildred has been deported from Zimbabwe after being categorized by the government as a prohibited immigrant.
9. The ____________________ Ahmed Ouyahia has said the number of people killed in an earthquake in the north of the country has risen to at least 450.
10. The ____________________ Kofi Annan has named Sergio Vieira de Mello as the ____________________ for an initial four months period.

Unit 10

Massage

Part One Before You Listen

I. Think and answer

1. Generally, when will a person consider having a massage?
2. Have you been massaged? If so, could you tell us about your experience?
3. Nowadays massage can also be used as a therapy to help those who have cancer. Can you guess why?
4. Do you know any other therapies to treat cancer? And what are they?

II. Make your prediction

Browse through all the information offered in this unit and predict the main idea of Text One and Text Two by choosing from a, b, c and d. You may choose more than one answer to indicate your prediction.

Text One

a. Celeste was turned away by her massage therapist after her illness had been diagnosed as cancer.

b. Many cancer patients experienced unfair treatment in the society.

c. To a certain degree, cancer patients need massage more than those who are healthy.

d. According to some experts, massage can even cure cancer.

Text Two

a. M. D. Anderson Cancer Center provides several complementary therapies including massage, which have been accepted by most cancer patients.

b. Massage therapy is now considered as an important complementary therapy for its effectiveness and popularity with cancer patients.

c. According to research by M. D. Anderson, massage is an efficient way to reduce side effects caused by conventional therapies but some cancer patients don't like it.

d. M. D. Anderson Cancer Center has found an ancient therapy even more effective than massage.

Part Two Listen Now

Text One

I. Words and expressions

therapist /'θerəpɪst/ *n.* (特定治疗法的)治疗专家
alleviate /ə'li:vɪeɪt/ *v.* 减轻痛苦
diagnose /'daɪəgnəuz/ *v.* 诊断
nausea /'nɔ:zɪə/ *n.* 恶心，反胃
malignant /mə'lɪgnənt/ *adj.* 恶性的
tumor /'tʃu:mə/ *n.* 肿瘤
the University of Texas Medical Center 得克萨斯大学医学中心
the M. D. Anderson Cancer Center M. D. 安德森癌症中心

II. Listen to confirm or to adjust

Listen and find out if your expectations are the same as or different from what you hear. If different, find the correct one or ones from ***Make your prediction****.*

III. Listen and choose the best answer to each question you hear.

1. a. It belongs to the University of Texas Medical Center.
   b. It is located in Houston, the US.
   c. It only provides therapies which are aimed at curing cancer.
   d. Massage therapists are available there almost every day.
2. a. Her family was not afraid of talking about her disease.
   b. Her massage therapist was very glad to provide service for her.

c. She gave up massage at last.
d. None of the above.

3. a. As long as massage therapists don't touch the cancer area.
   b. As long as massage therapists accept some relevant training.
   c. As long as massage therapists get the permission of cancer patients.
   d. As long as massage therapists are experienced.

IV. Listen and fill in the following blanks.

1. Celeste is a ________________________ in massage and thinks that it gives her hope that ______________________________ in spite of the tumor in her throat.
2. Celeste's experience shows that some massage therapists are worried that massage may ______________________________ if they provide services to cancer patients. Considering this, the M. D. Cancer Center is now working with massage therapists in Houston to ________________________________ and convince them that they can do it if they are careful enough.
3. Curtis, a ________________ massage therapist, believes cancer patients need massage _________________________ healthy people because they are suffering from fatigue, nausea, _________________________, and massage can relieve the stress and ________ ______________.

Text Two

I. Words and expressions

chemotherapy /ˌkeməʊˈθerəpɪ/ *n.* 化疗
debilitate /dɪˈbɪlɪteɪt/ *v.* 使虚弱
testimony /ˈtestɪmənɪ/ *n.* 证据；证明
efficacy /ˈefɪkəsɪ/ *n.* 功效；灵验
malady /ˈmælədɪ/ *n.* 疾病；病状

II. Listen to confirm or to adjust

Listen and find out if your expectations are the same as or different from what you hear. If different, find the correct one or ones from ***Make your prediction****.*

III. Listen and answer the following questions.

1. What is the M. D. Anderson Cancer Center known for?

____

2. Why is massage a complementary therapy instead of an alternative one?

____

3. How does M. D. Anderson prove that massage is efficient to reduce side effects?

____

4. Why is M. D. Anderson working with a university in Shanghai, China?

____

IV. Listen and decide whether the following statements are true (T) or false (F).

1. M. D. Anderson provides massage and other non-standard therapies mainly because they prove to be effective. T ☐ F ☐
2. At M. D. Anderson, 80% of the cancer patients accept some type of non-standard therapy to get spiritual relief. T ☐ F ☐
3. In addition to massage therapy, the M. D. Anderson Cancer Center introduces many other complementary therapies such as acupuncture, special diet and exercise programs and herbal medicines. T ☐ F ☐
4. Both chemotherapy and radiation are conventional therapies and usually cause side effects. T ☐ F ☐
5. Massage therapy proves important and efficient but it hasn't been fully recognized by the American Cancer Society. T ☐ F ☐

Part Three Look at This

新闻中常见的医疗词汇

大多数英语学习者在听英语新闻，特别是科技新闻时，感到很困难，甚至会抱怨说，这类新闻里有大量的专业术语，要记住它们根本是“不可能的任务”。其实，新闻中使用的专业术语并不如我们想像的那么多。如果我们留心总结的话，会发现有一部分词语是经常出现的，掌握这些词语，对提高我们的听力水平有很大的帮助。以本课为例，cancer，tumor，therapy，treatment 和 diagnose 这几个词在医疗新闻中就经常听到。关于此类新闻中出现的词汇，我们在这里作个小小的总结：

1. 疾病的名称

除"感冒"、"发烧"这些常见疾病名称，一般经常出现的还有：

AIDS/HIV (艾滋病/艾滋病毒)；arthritis (关节炎)；cholera (霍乱)；coronary heart disease (冠心病)；diabetes (糖尿病)；flu (流感)； fracture (骨折)；heart disease/attack (心脏病/心脏病发作)；high blood pressure (高血压)；insomnia (失眠症)；measles (麻疹)；obesity (肥胖症)；Parkinson's disease (帕金森氏病)；pneumonic plague (肺鼠疫)；smallpox (天花)；stroke (中风)；TB (tuberculosis, 结核病)

近来常听到的还有：

avian flu/avian influenza/bird flu (禽流感)；dengue fever (登革热)；mad cow disease (疯牛病)；SARS (非典)

2. 其他和疾病有关的词汇

ailment (不适，小病痛)；trauma (外伤)；(anti-)virus ([抗]病毒)；outbreak ([疾病等的]爆发)；insulin (胰岛素)；stem cell (干细胞)；symptom (症状)

还有一些词，我们要留意它们的不同词性：

1) circulate *v.* (血液等)循环
   circulation *n.* 循环
2) dose *n.* 剂量；一剂
   dosage *n.* (按剂量的)给药；(一次)一剂
3) epidemic *adj.* 流行性的
   n. 流行病
4) gene *n.* 基因
   genetic *adj.* 遗传学的
5) immune *adj.* 免疫的；有免疫力的
   immunity *n.* 免疫力
   immunize *v.* 使免疫
6) infect *v.* 传染；感染
   infection *n.* 传染；传染病
   infectious *adj.* 传染的；传染性的
7) vaccine *n.* 疫苗
   vaccinate *v.* 给……接种疫苗
   vaccination *n.* 接种
8) molecule *n.* 分子
   molecular *adj.* 分子的
9) toxin *n.* 毒素
   toxic *adj.* 有毒的
10) obese *adj.* 肥胖的
    obesity *n.* 过度肥胖；肥胖症

3. 和身体/器官有关的名词

head；shoulder；chest；arm；elbow；wrist；fist；breast；stomach；hip；thigh；knee; calf (腿肚)；ankle；heel；foot；heart；lung；liver；backbone (脊骨)；blood vessel (血管)

总之，平时听新闻时不断地总结经常出现的专业词汇，能帮助我们更好地理解专业性较强的听力材料。

Part Four Here's More

Exercise One

You will hear four statements. Listen and write down the names of the diseases mentioned in them.

1. ______
2. ______
3. ______
4. ______

Exercise Two

Listen and write down the definitions of the diseases you hear.

1. Flu is ______.
2. Obesity is ______.
3. Insomnia is ______.
4. Diabetes is ______.
5. AIDS is ______
______.
6. Heart attack is ______
______.
7. TB or tuberculosis is ______.

Unit 11 Sports Events

Part One Before You Listen

I. Think and answer

1. What sports activities do you often take part in?
2. Name some sports events that captivate people around the globe.
3. What benefits do you think sports activities can bring to people?
4. How enthusiastically are today's people fond of sports and proud of their athlete stars?

II. Make your prediction

Browse through all the information offered in this unit and predict the main idea of Text One and Text Two by choosing from a, b, c and d. You may choose more than one answer to indicate your prediction.

Text One

a. Opening ceremony of the 20th Winter Olympics.
b. Origin of Olympics.
c. Development of Olympics.
d. Host of 2008 Olympics.

Text Two

a. Award winners of 2006 World Cup Germany.
b. 2006 World Cup final.
c. 2006 World Cup opening gala.
d. Germany ousted from 2006 World Cup final.

Part Two Listen Now

Text One

I. Words and expressions

legend /ˈledʒənd/ *n.* 传奇；传奇式人物
fiery /ˈfaɪərɪ/ *adj.* 燃烧的，似火的
festivity /fesˈtɪvətɪ/ *n.* 欢庆，庆典
pageantry /ˈpædʒəntrɪ/ *n.* 壮观；盛况
dope /dəʊp/ *v.* 使……服麻醉品，服用兴奋剂
tenor /ˈtenə/ *n.* 男高音歌手
cauldron /ˈkɔːldrən/ *n.* (煮汤用的) 大锅；主火炬塔
vie /vaɪ/ *v.* 竞争
cap off 使达到顶峰；使圆满完成

II. Listen to confirm or to adjust

Listen and find out if your expectations are the same as or different from what you hear. If different, find the correct one or ones from ***Make your prediction****.*

III. Listen and choose the best answer to each question you hear.

1. a. Laura Bush.
   b. Jacques Rogge.
   c. John Lennon.
   d. Luciano Pavarotti.

2. a. More than 2, 600.
   b. More than 4, 700.
   c. More than 35, 000.
   d. More than 15, 000.

3. a. Performance of Italian tenor Luciano Pavarotti.
   b. Performance of John Lennon's wife and Peter Gabriel.
   c. Performance of the President of the Italian Republic.
   d. Performance of the former cross country skier.

4. a. Its final bearer was a former cross country skier from Italy.
   b. It was the tallest-ever torch.
   c. It lit the tallest-ever Olympic cauldron.
   d. The fire was seen throughout the city during the competition.

IV. Listen and fill in the following blanks.

1. Athletes from more than ____________________ marched into the stadium accompanied by ____________________ from the 1970s and 1980s.
2. Athletes should compete in the spirit of ________________, ________________ and ____________________, and above all, compete cleanly by ____________.
3. The final torch bearer lit the tallest-ever Olympic cauldron, which rises to ________________. It will be seen throughout the city during the ____________ days of competition, as athletes vie for ____________ gold medals in ____________ sports.
4. The Olympics are being protected by unprecedented security, which includes some 15,000 ________________ and a ________________ backed up by NATO ________________.

Text Two

I. Words and expressions

draw /drɔː/ *n.* 平局，和局
net /net/ *n.* (足球、曲棍球等的)球门网
quarterfinal /ˌkwɔːtəˈfaɪnəl/ *n.* 四分之一决赛
shoot-out /ˈʃuːtaʊt/ *n.* 点球大战
blast /blaːst/ *v.* 爆破，发射
penalty /ˈpenəltɪ/ kick 罚(点)球

II. Listen to confirm or to adjust

Listen and find out if your expectations are the same as or different from what you hear. If different, find the correct one or ones from ***Make your prediction****.*

III. Listen and decide whether the following statements are true (T) or false (F).

1. Italy had won every match to Germany in every World Cup. *T* ☐ *F* ☐
2. Both Italy and Germany were scoreless during the 90 minutes match and 30 minutes of extra time. *T* ☐ *F* ☐
3. Italy won its semifinal against Germany on penalty kicks. *T* ☐ *F* ☐
4. Penalty kicks always depend on luck according to the Italian coach. *T* ☐ *F* ☐
5. The Germans will play for third place on Saturday against either France or Portugal. *T* ☐ *F* ☐

IV. Listen and answer the following questions.

1. How did Germany play against Italy during the 90 minutes of the match and what was the result then?
   ____
2. When did Italy shoot during the match?
   ____
3. Why was the Italian coach proud of his team?
   ____
4. Why was the German coach also proud of his team despite the defeat?
   ____

Part Three Look at This

体育新闻报道中的术语

体育新闻报道中，常常会出现一些术语，如果对它们一无所知，听者可能会听得云里雾里，不知所云。要熟悉这些术语没什么捷径可走，只有踏实学习：一是通过阅读积累这方面的词汇，二要多进行听力实践，一个单词反复听上5至6遍后想忘也忘不了。

下面是一些和体育有关的术语。

1. 重大国际赛事

Olympics（国际奥林匹克运动会）；World Cup（世界杯足球赛）；Formula 1（一级方程式赛车）；Asian Games（亚运会）；World Rally Championship（世界拉力锦标赛）；Master Cup（网球大师杯赛）；Thomas Uber Cup（汤尤杯羽毛球锦标赛）；World Baseball Classic（世界棒球经典赛）；Wimbledon Tennis Tournament（温布尔顿网球锦标赛）；All-Star Basketball Games（全明星篮球赛）；IAAF Golden League（国际田径黄金联赛）

2. 国际体育组织

International Olympic Committee （IOC）国际奥林匹克委员会

Fédération Internationale de Football Association （FIFA）国际足联

International Association of Athletics Federations （IAAF）国际田联

International Badminton Federation （IBF）国际羽联

International Table Tennis Federation （ITTF）国际乒联

International Basketball Federation （IBAF）国际篮联

National Basketball Association （NBA）全美篮球协会

World Boxing Association （WBA）世界拳击协会

3. 球类运动

football（足球）；rugby（橄榄球）；basketball（篮球）；volleyball（排球）；tennis（网球）；table tennis（乒乓球）；badminton（羽毛球）；baseball（棒球）；golf（高尔夫球）；cricket（板球）；hockey（曲棍球）；ice hockey（冰球）

4. 足球术语

goalkeeper（守门员）；score（得分）；penalty kick（罚点球）；penalty spot（罚球点）；extra playing time（加时赛）；forward/striker（前锋）；midfielder（中场队员）；fullback（后卫）；ball handling（运球）；attack（进攻）；defend（防守）；shot（射门）；beat（打败，战胜）；qualifier（资格赛）；draw/tie（平局）；final（决赛）；semifinal（半决赛）；breakaway（过人、突围）；curl the free kick（弧线任意球）；header（头球）；corner kick（角球）；half（半场）；long ball（长传）；pitch/field（足球场地）；red/yellow card（红/黄牌）；shootout（点球决胜负）；penalty zone（禁区）

5. 篮球术语

playing court（球场）；lane place line（分位线）；free throw line（罚球线）；side line（边线）；free throw lane（罚球区）；center line（中线）；three-point line（三分线）；end line（端线）；restricted area（限制区）；boundary line （界线）；lane place（位置区）；front court（前场）；neutral zone（中立区）；mid court（中场）；team bench（球队席）；back court （后

场）；basket post（篮架支柱）；center circle（中圈）；ring（篮圈）；own basket（本方球篮）；net（篮网）；opponent's basket（对方球篮）；backboard（篮板）；foul markers（犯规次数牌）；team foul marker（全队犯规标志）；basket support（篮架）；substitute bench（替补队员席）；team bench areas（球队席区域）；whistle（哨）；dimension of the court（球场面积）；three-point field goal areas（三分投篮区）

6. 排球术语

volleyball court（排球场地）；court（一方场区）；opponent's court（对方场区）；service area（发球区）；attack line（进攻线）；official's tribune（裁判台）；vertical rod（标志杆）；back line（端线）；back zone（后区）；attack zone（进攻区）

7. 田径比赛

track（跑道）；field（田赛场地）；scoreboard（成绩公布牌）；hammer throw（掷链球）；javelin throw（掷标枪）；discus throw（掷铁饼）；shot put（推铅球）；pole vault（撑竿跳高）；high jump（跳高）；long jump（跳远）；triple jump（三级跳远）；victory rostrum（领奖台）；starting point（起跑点）；finish line（终点线）；sprint（短跑）；middle/long distance race（中/长跑）；race walking（竞走）；hurdles（跨栏）；relay（接力）；steeplechase（障碍赛）；cross-country race（越野赛）；marathon（马拉松）

对于体育新闻感兴趣的同学还可以积累更多体育项目的专门术语。

Part Four Here's More

Exercise

Listen and complete the following table.

Development of the FIFA World Cup	
Initiators	A group of (1) ________________, led by Jules Rimet.
First competition	Held in Uruguay in (2) ________.
During World War II	Competition stopped for (3) ________.
Since 1958	Held alternately in (4) ________________ and (5) ________ ________.
In 1950	The (6) ________________ defeated England.

In 1966	(7) ____________________ defeated Italy.
In (8) _______	Cameroon emerged.
In 1990	Cameroon defeated (9) ________ in the opening match.
In 1998	Over (10) _________ people watched the France tournament, including approximately (11) _________ for the final alone, while over (12) ________ people flocked to watch the (13) ________ matches in the French stadium.
In 2002	(14) ____________________ co-hosted the 2002 edition.

Unit 12 Around the World

Part One Before You Listen

I. Think and answer

1. What do you know about the insurgency in Iraq after the US-led war against it?
2. What do you know about the tension and peace talk between Israelis and Palestinians?
3. Have you heard of mad cow disease? How will people be affected if they eat the infected meat?
4. What may cause flooding and what may flooding cause?
5. What do you know about the wildfire in Australia?

II. Make your prediction

Browse through all the information offered in this unit and predict the main idea of Text One and Text Two by choosing from a, b, c and d. You may choose more than one answer to indicate your prediction.

Text One

a. Killings in Baghdad.
b. Killings in Israel and Palestine.
c. Mad cow disease in Canada.
d. Killings in Canada.

Text Two

a. Flood in several countries.
b. Earthquake in Tokyo.

c. Wildfire in Australia.

d. Mad cow disease in Canada.

Part Two Listen Now

Text One

I. Words and expressions

insurgent /ɪnˈsɜːdʒənt/ *n.* 叛乱者
deter /dɪˈtɜː/ *v.* 制止
mortar /ˈmɔːtə/ *n.* 迫击炮
exchange /ɪksˈtʃeɪndʒ/ *n.* 交火
late /leɪt/ *adj.* 已故的
positive /ˈpɒzətɪv/ *adj.* 阳性的
bovine /ˈbəʊvaɪn/ *adj.* 牛的
encephalopathy /enˌsefəˈlɒpəθɪ/ *n.* 脑疾
Ali al-Haidri 阿里 · 海德里（人名）
Yasser Arafat 亚西尔 · 阿拉法特（人名）
Alberta /ælˈbɜːtə/ 阿尔伯达省（加拿大）

II. Listen to confirm or to adjust

Listen and find out if your expectations are the same as or different from what you hear. If different, find the correct one or ones from ***Make your prediction****.*

III. Listen and choose the best answer to each question you hear.

1. a. 1.
   b. 2.
   c. 11.
   d. 12.

2. a. Monday.
   b. Tuesday.
   c. Wednesday.
   d. Thursday.

3. a. Because no case of mad cow disease has been found in over a decade.
   b. Because eating meat from infected animals will not do any harm to the people.
   c. Because no part of the infected animal entered the human food or animal feed systems.
   d. Because Canadians eat imported beef only.

IV. Listen and complete the following table.

	Item 1	Item 2	Item 3
Who/Whom?	Insurgents.	Seven Palestinians.	Officials.
What?	Carried out new (1) ________.	Were killed by Israeli tank fire.	Announced a new case of (5)________.
When?	Tuesday.	(3) __________.	Sunday.
Where?	(2) __________.	In the Middle East/In North Gaza.	(6)___________.
Why/How?	Some in a road ambush and some with a truck bomb.	In response to a Palestinian (4) _________ attack on an Israeli target.	

Text Two

I. Words and expressions

torrential /tɒ'renʃəl/ *adj.* 猛烈的
lash /læʃ/ *v.* 鞭打
landslide /'lændslaɪd/ *n.* 山崩
rainfall /'reɪnfɔːl/ *n.* 降雨
displace /dɪs'pleɪs/ *v.* 使流离失所
ravage /'rævɪdʒ/ *v.* 破坏

acre /ˈeɪkə/ *n.* 英亩
fuel /fjʊəl/ *v.* 加燃料
stepped-up /ˈsteptʌp/ *adj.* 加强的
in excess of 超过
São Paulo /ˈsaʊŋˈpaʊlʊ/ 圣保罗（巴西东南部城市）
Costa Rica /ˌkɒstəˈriːkə/ 哥斯达黎加（拉丁美洲国家）

II. Listen to confirm or to adjust

*Listen and find out if your expectations are the same as or different from what you hear. If different, find the correct one or ones from **Make your prediction**.*

III. Listen and decide whether the following statements are true (T) or false (F).

1. Severe flooding was reported in the UK only. *T* ☐ *F* ☐
2. Many people lost their homes because of heavy rains along the Atlantic coast. *T* ☐ *F* ☐
3. Firefighters have given up fighting against the wildfire in Australia. *T* ☐ *F* ☐
4. The wildfire has killed hundreds of thousands of people already. *T* ☐ *F* ☐
5. The temperature was very high where the wildfire took place. *T* ☐ *F* ☐
6. Canada announced a new case of mad cow disease but it posed no danger to consumers. *T* ☐ *F* ☐

IV. Listen and complete the answers to the following questions.

1. How bad was the flooding in northwestern England?
   It was the worst in ________________________.
2. What caused severe flooding in Brazil?
   Torrential ________________________.
3. How many people were killed in the wildfire in South Australia?
   ________________________ at least.

4. When did the wildfire break out?

______________________.

5. How many cases of mad cow disease have been found in Canada in less than a month?

______________________.

Part Three Look at This

新闻的五要素（5Ws）

对英语学习者而言，新闻语速快，信息量大，不易听懂。但是了解了新闻的特点，抓住新闻的五要素后就不会再感到那么难了。什么是新闻的五要素？怎样抓住这五要素呢？

首先，所谓新闻的五要素(英文称作5Ws)即：

1. 发生了什么？（**What**）
2. 谁使之发生，或发生在谁身上？（**Who/Whom**）
3. 什么时候发生的？（**When**）
4. 什么地方发生的？（**Where**）
5. 为什么发生，或怎样发生的？（**Why/How**）

那么，如何抓住这五要素呢？第一，要有意识地带着这五个问题去听新闻，有的放矢地捕捉信息；第二，重点听清新闻的开头，因为很多新闻报道的信息呈倒三角形分布，最重要的信息放在最开头，接下来是次重要的信息，再接下来是更为次要的信息，最后可能是一些补充性的背景信息。因此这五个要素往往出现在新闻报道的头两句，这就意味着我们必须一开始就全神贯注，从第一二句话中捕捉五要素。如Text One中第一则新闻的第一句话：

First stop, Iraq — where insurgents carried out new attacks Tuesday.

这句话就包含了几个要素：

Where — Iraq

Who — insurgents

What — carried out new attacks

When — Tuesday

下面我们听几则新闻，做一些针对性的练习。

Part Four Here's More

Exercise One

Listen twice and fill in the following blanks.

A report in a Spanish newspaper says (1) ________________ had (2)________________ plans for a terrorist (3)________________ on (4) ________________'s Grand Central Station.

Exercise Two

Listen three times and answer the following questions.

1. What happened?

   ____

2. Where did it happen?

   ____

3. When did it happen?

   ____

4. To whom did it happen?

   ____

Exercise Three

Listen three times and supply the basic information.

1. Who?

   A ________________ girl.

2. Did what?

   She won the right to ________________ full Islamic ________________ at school.

3. Where?

   At her ________________ school.

4. When did the rule come out?

   ________________.

Exercise Four

Listen twice and decide whether the following statements are true (T) or false (F).

1. The news is about a plane crash in Mexico. *T* ☐ *F* ☐
2. 80 people have been killed in the accident. *T* ☐ *F* ☐
3. The cause to the accident remains unknown. *T* ☐ *F* ☐

Exercise Five

Listen twice and complete the following table.

What happened?	A suicide (1) ____________________.
When did it happen?	(2) ________________.
How many people were killed?	(3) At least __________________.
How many people were injured?	More than (4) ______________.
Where did it happen?	At a police (5) _________ center (6) _________ of Baghdad.

Unit 13

A Different Voice

Part One Before You Listen

I. Think and answer

1. When did some EU countries say goodbye to their old national currencies?
2. Has Britain adopted the euro as its national currency? Why or why not?
3. Where can tourists and alike use euro in UK?
4. Under what circumstances would workers go on a strike?
5. What impact will farming automation have on farm workers?

II. Make your prediction

Browse through all the information offered in this unit and predict the main idea of Text One and Text Two by choosing from a, b, c and d. You may choose more than one answer to indicate your prediction.

Text One

a. The International Eisteddfod in Llangollen.
b. Tourists' reaction to the first euro zone in UK.
c. Local businesses' reaction to the first euro zone in UK.
d. Strikes against the first euro zone in UK.

Text Two

a. Californian winery owners go on a strike against the government.
b. Californian wine workers go on a strike against the winery owners.
c. Californian wine workers are happy about the coming grape harvest.
d. Californian winery owners are worried about the coming grape harvest.

Part Two Listen Now

Text One

I. Words and expressions

eisteddfod /aɪs'tedvɒd/ *n.* 威尔士诗歌音乐比赛年会
foot-and-mouth /'fʊtən'maʊθ/ *n.* 口蹄疫
front line 前线，第一线
put (something) on the map 使……闻名
Llangollen 兰格伦（英国威尔士北部小镇）

II. Listen to confirm or to adjust

Listen and find out if your expectations are the same as or different from what you hear. If different, find the correct one or ones from ***Make your prediction****.*

III. Listen and decide whether the following statements are true (T) or false(F).

1. Only the euro will be accepted at the festival but not sterling. *T* ☐ *F* ☐
2. Not everyone is happy about the euro zone. *T* ☐ *F* ☐
3. The annual music festival attracts people from all over the world and aims to celebrate cultural diversity. *T* ☐ *F* ☐
4. European tourists feel confused about banks and shops taking the euro. *T* ☐ *F* ☐

IV. Listen and fill in the following blanks.

Llangollen has declared itself a euro zone while it holds its (1) __________ music festival. For (2) __________, and more, this Welsh hillside town has drawn dancers, singers, and musicians from all over the globe for an (3) __________ celebration of cultural diversity. (4) __________ people will be here this week from more than 40 countries. European tourists have come here with their new common currency and are (5) __________ that most banks, shops and restaurants are taking it. And if the euro zone helps bring in the tourists, most (6) __________ will be happy with it.

Text Two

I. Words and expressions

proposal /prəʊ'pəʊzəl/ *n.* 提议
gondola /'gɒndələ/ *n.* 吊舱
hopper /'hɒpə/ *n.* 给料漏斗；布料器
vintage /'vɪntɪdʒ/ *n.* 陈酿
winery /'waɪnərɪ/ *n.* 酿酒厂
picket /'pɪkɪt/ *n.* 纠察队

II. Listen to confirm or to adjust

Listen and find out if your expectations are the same as or different from what you hear. If different, find the correct one or ones from ***Make your prediction****.*

III. Listen and choose the best answer to each of the following questions.

1. When did the Californian wine workers begin the strike?
   a. This week.
   b. Last week.
   c. Six weeks ago.
   d. Seven weeks ago.

2. Why did the workers go on strike?
   a. The winery owners propose to cut their wages.
   b. The winery owners propose to cut their wages and benefits.
   c. The winery owners propose to fire them.
   d. The winery owners propose to use non-union workers.

3. Which of the following can be inferred from the news?
   a. The harvest was severely affected by the strike.
   b. The union workers are bound to win their battle against their employers.
   c. The strike went ahead successfully.
   d. The strike didn't seem to disturb winery owners very much.

IV. Listen and fill in the following blanks.

This week, Californian wine workers vote on a (1) ____________ proposal from winery owners. The workers have now been on (2) ____________ for six weeks. The contract proposal calls for cuts in wages and cuts in (3) ____________. The prospects for rank and file approval seem (4) ____________. A central issue of the strike is the (5) ____________ well-being of the California wine industry. William Drummond reports.

A gondola containing tons of freshly picked Chardonnay grapes is dumped into a hopper as the process begins for bottling the 1986 vintage. The harvest has continued despite the fact that (6) ____ ____________________________________ in Northern and Central California. Relying on automated plants and non-union labor, members of the Winery Owners' Association have succeeded in carrying on what looks like business is usual. But out on picket line, union worker Pat Scoley is (7)_________________________.

"I guess they're doing all right. If they aren't, they want us to think they are. I hope to hell they aren't, between you and me."

Part Three Look at This

巧妙利用话语重复　轻松理解新闻特写

在特写类新闻(feature)中，常常会直接引用有关人士的讲话，而这些话语片段往往成为外语学习者理解上的难点，因为讲话的人各种各样，来自不同的阶层和行业，年龄性别各异，教育程度不一，他们的话在语音语调、遣词造句以及语篇构成上都存在个体差异，例如黑人英语的双重否定、东南亚英语的口音、政府官员的外交辞令等等。因此，初学者往往认为这一类新闻报道很难听懂。

有趣的是，很多新闻特写似乎考虑到引用不同发言给听众造成的困难，在直接引用之前往往预备了一些概括性的陈述，这种陈述通常是以间接引语的形式出现的。

本课的 Text One 和 Text Two 中都有此类例子。如 Text One 在引用游客讲话之前有这样一个概括性的转述：European tourists have come here with their new common currency, and are delighted that most banks, shops and restaurants are taking it.

我们可以比较一下以上的叙述和接下来直接引用的游客讲话：

Man: It will be better for tourists.

Woman 2: If I bring euros, it saves me rushing into a bank to pick up some money.

不难看出转述和直接引语在内容上有相当程度的重复性。直接引语往往是之前转述的继承和扩展，所以听懂播音员的间接陈述，可以大大帮助我们听懂之后播放的各类人士的讲话。

下面我们针对新闻特写的这个特点做几个练习。

Here's More

Exercise One

I. Listen and choose between a and b on the viewpoint of the campaigner and a local resident on the first euro zone in UK.

1. The campaigner (the first speaker) is saying ________ to the use of euro.
   a. yes
   b. no

2. The local resident (the third speaker) is ________ about Llangollen being the first euro zone in UK.
   a. happy
   b. upset

II. Listen and fill in the following blanks.

1. Anti-euro campaigners suspect this experiment has less to do with pleasing the tourists, than prompting an unpopular ________________________, ditching the pound.
2. This essentially cultural event would not have attracted the support of the Foreign Office, Treasury, and European Commission unless there was, at the very least, a subtle political agenda. What critics of the government suspect, once again, is that ________________ ____.

Exercise Two

Listen twice and decide whether the following statements are true (T) or false (F).

1. The Union contract expired at a time when wine makers usually need all the help they can get. *T* ☐ *F* ☐
2. Only a few wineries have been automated so the owners have to rely heavily on the workers. *T* ☐ *F* ☐
3. Owner Peter Mondaby doesn't seem much disturbed by the strike. *T* ☐ *F* ☐

Exercise Three

Listen twice and fill in the following blanks.

Wages for workers in the winery industry range from around (1) ______________ ______________________________. The union was willing to give up a slight reduction in wages, but refused to accept cuts in (2) ______________________________________. The employers reportedly want a twenty percent reduction in the wages and benefits package. Winery owners say the union has to recognize that (3) ______________________________ __________________.

"Not only is your gross down; the competition has forced us to increase marketing and advertising, which is further eroding whatever margin was there."

Unit 14

Abolishing Juvenile Death Penalty

Part One Before You Listen

I. Think and answer

1. What do you think of capital punishment? Do you support it or oppose it?
2. Recently, the juvenile crime rate is sharply increasing in the world. What do you think is the main cause of it?
3. In your opinion, what measures should be taken to prevent juvenile crime?

II. Make your prediction

Browse through all the information offered in this unit and predict the main idea of Text One and Text Two by choosing from a, b, c and d. You may choose more than one answer to indicate your prediction.

Text One

a. The abolishment of the juvenile death penalty in the US.
b. Death penalty advocates' opinions and reactions.
c. The influence on the country after the juvenile death penalty is abolished.
d. A justice's efforts to abolish the death penalty.

Text Two

a. The opinions of the fathers of two juvenile crime victims.
b. Some arguments against the abolishment of the juvenile death penalty.
c. The number of juvenile criminals who had been sentenced to death.
d. A trend on the US Supreme Court in recent years.

Part Two Listen Now

Text One

I. Words and expressions

penalty /ˈpenəltɪ/ *n.* 刑罚
unconstitutional /ˈʌnˌkɒnstɪˈtjuːʃənəl/ *adj.* 违反宪法的
execute /ˈeksɪkjuːt/ *v.* 将……处死
execution /ˌeksɪˈkjuːʃən/ *n.* 处死
juvenile /ˈdʒuːvənaɪl/ *adj.* 少年的；适合青少年的
justice /ˈdʒʌstɪs/ *n.* 法官；司法
overwhelming /ˌəʊvəˈhwelmɪŋ/ *adj.* 呈压倒之势的
categorically /ˌkætɪˈgɒrɪkəlɪ/ *adv.* 绝对地
culpable /ˈkʌlpəbl/ *adj.* 负有责任的；有罪的
maturity /məˈtjʊərətɪ/ *n.* 成熟
offender /əˈfendə/ *n.* 违法者，罪犯
impose /ɪmˈpəʊz/ *v.* 把……强加于
blameworthiness /ˈbleɪmˌwɜːðɪnɪs/ *n.* 该受责备
outlaw /ˈaʊtlɔː/ *v.* 宣布……为不合法；禁止
dwindle /ˈdwɪndl/ *v.* 缩小；减少
handful /ˈhændfʊl/ *n.* 少量；少数
capital punishment 死刑，极刑
US Supreme Court 美国最高法院
high court 高等法院

II. Listen to confirm or to adjust

*Listen and find out if your expectations are the same as or different from what you hear. If different, find the correct one or ones from **Make your prediction**.*

III. Listen and choose the best answer to complete each of the following statements.

1. By a vote of ________, the high court outlawed the execution of juvenile criminals.

a. five to two
b. four to five
c. fifty to four
d. five to four

2. Reactions from the capital punishment opponents are ________.
   a. quick and positive
   b. slow but positive
   c. swift but not positive
   d. slow and negative

3. A group called the Juvenile Law Center ________ the juvenile death penalty.
   a. supports
   b. opposes
   c. argues for
   d. is neutral in terms of

4. Due to the abolishment of the juvenile death penalty in the US, ________ juvenile murderers won't be executed.
   a. 17
   b. 70
   c. more than 17
   d. more than 70

5. According to the news, ________ hasn't (haven't) abolished juvenile executions yet.
   a. Pakistan
   b. Iran
   c. Saudi Arabia
   d. All of thc above.

IV. Listen and fill in the following blanks.

Here are the opinions of two juvenile death penalty opponents:

Justice Anthony Kennedy's arguments:

- An overwhelming weight of (1) ________________________ has moved against the death penalty.
- Juvenile criminals are less culpable than (2) ______________________ because of their lack of (3) __________ and (4) ________________.

Marsha Levick's argument:

- Capital punishment should not be applied to juvenile offenders who usually do not have adult blameworthiness, adult culpability or (5) ____________________ ______.

Text Two

I. Words and expressions

dissent /dɪˈsent/ *v.* 不同意，持异议
eligible /ˈelɪdʒəbl/ *adj.* 符合被选中条件的
severity /sɪˈverətɪ/ *n.* 严重性
offense /əˈfens/ *n.* 犯法（行为）
felony /ˈfelənɪ/ *n.* 重罪
reinstate /ˌriːɪnˈsteɪt/ *v.* 恢复
restrict /rɪˈstrɪkt/ *v.* 限制；限定
retard /rɪˈtɑːd/ *v.* 阻止；妨碍

II. Listen to confirm or to adjust

Listen and find out if your expectations are the same as or different from what you hear. If different, find the correct one or ones from ***Make your prediction****.*

III. Listen and answer the following questions.

1. At what age is an American entitled to drink, vote and serve in the military?

   ____

2. How did the families who had lost their loved ones to juvenile murderers react to the news?

   ____

3. How many juvenile criminals have been executed since 1976?

   ____

4. What is the trend on the Supreme Court in recent years?

   ____

IV. Listen and decide whether the following statements are true (T) or false (F).

1. Richard Dieter, the executive director of the Death Penalty Information Center, opposed Justice Kennedy's opinion. *T* ☐ *F* ☐
2. Justice Sandra Day O'Connor argued that juvenile criminals should be put to death depending on the severity of the crime. *T* ☐ *F* ☐

3. All the juvenile murderers had committed more than one serious crime before they were caught. *T* ☐ *F* ☐
4. The decision of abolishing the juvenile death penalty probably has been affected by a trend on the Supreme Court in recent years. *T* ☐ *F* ☐
5. In the US, mentally retarded criminals shouldn't be executed because it is considered unconstitutional. *T* ☐ *F* ☐

Part Three Look at This

关注长句中的连词　避免听了后半句忘了前半句

新闻报道在用词和句子结构上更偏向书面语，因此我们在听新闻时经常会听到长长的句子。本单元的课文中有许多这样的例子，请看以下摘自本单元的例句：

1. By a vote of five to four, the high court ruled that it is now unconstitutional to execute criminals who were younger than 18 when they committed their crimes.
2. Justice Kennedy also wrote that American society views juveniles as, in his words, "categorically less culpable than the average criminal" because of their lack of maturity and emotional stability.

长句之所以长，原因之一是从句套从句；另外，句子中出现多个介词短语、同位语短语或非谓语动词短语也是句子变长的原因。请看例句1，宾语从句里有定语从句，而定语从句又带了状语从句。再看例句2，宾语从句里带了三个介词短语。既然句子长和从句有关，那么我们应该关注那些连接从句的连词，因为它们点明了主从句之间的关系。同时，既然句子长和介词短语有关，那么我们也应该关注介词，因为通过它们，我们能弄清介词短语的意思及其在句子中的地位，它们往往起定语或状语的作用。当然，前提是句子中的主干——主语、谓语、宾语也不能遗漏。简言之，听长句时，关注连词、介词短语或非谓语动词短语等，化长为短，长句听起来就不会那么杂乱无章，没有头绪，以致前听后忘了。

另外我们还可以通过复述听到的长句子来提高听力理解，虽然较费时间，但效果会很明显。

本单元的话题和法律有关，因此我们列出了一些相关的词汇。

1. 有关法律法规制定的词汇

legal 法律的；法学的
constitution 宪法； written/unwritten constitution 成文 / 不成文宪法
justice 司法；judiciary 司法部；judicial power/official 司法权 / 官员

act 法令；法规
bill of rights 权利法案
criminal law 刑法
civil law 民法，包括：
family law 家庭法；property law 财产法；administrative law 行政法；labor law 劳动法；law of torts 民事侵权法；mercantile law 商业法；intellectual property law 知识产权法；contract law 合同法；company law 公司法

2. 有关各类犯罪的词汇
treason 叛国罪；murder 谋杀；espionage 间谍活动；arson 纵火；放火；poisoning 投毒; robbery 抢劫; theft 盗窃; burglary 入室盗窃; kidnapping 绑架; fraud 诈骗; forgery 伪造；corruption 贪污；腐败；bribery 贿赂；libel 诽谤；perjury 作伪证；sexual offence 性犯罪

3. 有关法庭的词汇
law court/court of law/legal court/court 法院；法庭
criminal court 刑事法庭
civil court 民事法庭
juvenile court 未成年人法庭；少年法庭
court of appeal 上诉法庭
judge 法官； magistrate/Justice of the Peace 地方法官
prosecute 起诉(*n.* prosecution)
the prosecution 原告方；prosecutor 起诉人；plaintiff 原告
the defense 被告方；defendant 被告
lawyer 律师
jury/jury panel 陪审团； juror 陪审员
legal advice/legal counseling 法律咨询
legal aid 法律援助
case 案件
witness 证人
accuse 控告 (*n.* accusation)
trial 审判；审讯
charge 指控；罪名
convict 定罪 (*n.* conviction)
abide by the law 守法
custody 拘留；监禁
evidence 证据
life sentence 无期徒刑
life imprisonment 终身监禁
retrial 复审；重审
plead guilty/not guilty 认罪 / 不认罪
give/reach/deliver a verdict 作出裁决
make/accept/reject an appeal 提出 / 接受 / 拒绝上诉

Here's More

Exercise

I. Listen and fill in the following blanks. (One word for each blank.)

1. She argued ________ ________ ________ those under 18 may be less culpable for their crimes than adults, they should still be eligible for the death penalty ____________ on the severity of the offense.
2. The Death Penalty Information Center says 22 criminals have been executed for crimes committed ________ they were 16 or 17 ________ the Supreme Court reinstated the death penalty in 1976.
3. As the UK cools down this week, parts of the US are again bracing themselves ________ rising heat and humidity levels ________ the latest heatwave spreads to the eastern US states.
4. At the age of 41, Joel Osteen is a religious superstar, ________ not only the more than 40,000 registered members of his church in Houston, ________ millions of people around the world ________ his televised ministry and his best-selling book, ________ ________ ________ ________ — *Seven Steps to Living at Your Full Potential.*
5. They say the bus was apparently racing a second bus to pick up passengers ________ at the next stop, ________ it was hit by the train.
6. Indonesian President Susilo Bambang Yudhoyono, ________ is on a state visit to Australia, has extended his condolences to the families of the seven men and two women ________ died, and says they will be awarded the Indonesian Medal of Honor.
7. It says people ________ food in areas ________ avian-flu outbreaks should wash hands frequently, and all surfaces and utensils ________ have been in contact with raw meat should be washed and disinfected.
8. The returned Chinese students all agree ________ their greatest challenge was the transition to a classroom ________ students ask questions, reply to questions, and state and defend points of view.
9. According to Mr. Cook, "One of the issues ________ the United States is confronting, ________ ________ of the situation in Iraq, is ________ Iraq clearly had nothing to do with 9/11 despite the administration's best efforts to kind of ally Iraq and 9/11 during the 2004 presidential election."

II. Listen to the above 9 sentences one by one. After hearing each sentence, pause the recording, repeat and try to write it down.

1. ____

____

2. ____

____

3. ____

____

4. ____

____

5. ____

____

6. ____

____

7. ____

____

8. ____

____

9. ____

____

Unit 15

Deep in Heat

Part One Before You Listen

I. Think and answer

1. What's the weather like today? How do you like it?
2. What's the highest temperature in summer in your area? How do you cope with the heatwave in summer?
3. How much is the average rainfall in your area?
4. Which place of the world is known for its monsoon seasons? What is it like in the monsoon season?

II. Make your prediction

Browse through all the information offered in this unit and predict the main idea of Text One and Text Two by choosing from a, b, c and d. You may choose more than one answer to indicate your prediction.

Text One

a. The scorching heat in USA.
b. The freezing cold in USA.
c. The pleasant summer along the coastline.
d. The soothing breeze brought by the sea.

Text Two

a. Monsoon in its full swing.
b. Monsoon on its way.
c. The disastrous effect of monsoon.
d. The cool weather in the monsoon season.

Part Two

Listen Now

Text One

I. Words and expressions

Fahrenheit /ˈfærənhaɪt/ *adj.* 华氏的
stretch /stretʃ/ *n.* 一段时间
triple-digit /ˈtrɪplˈdɪdʒɪt/ *adj.* 三位数的
Philadelphia /ˌfɪləˈdelfɪə/ 费城(美国宾夕法尼亚州东南部港市)
Baltimore /ˈbɔːltɪmɔː/ 巴尔的摩(美国马里兰州中北部港市)
Minneapolis /ˌmɪnɪˈæpəlɪs/ 明尼阿波利斯(美国明尼苏达州东南部城市)
North Dakota /dəˈkəʊtə/ 北达科他州(美国)
Bismarck /ˈbɪzmɑːk/ 俾斯麦(美国北达科他州首府)

II. Listen to confirm or to adjust

Listen and find out if your expectations are the same as or different from what you hear. If different, find the correct one or ones from ***Make your prediction****.*

III. Listen and choose the best answer to each of the following questions.

1. What's the weather like in the eastern part of USA?
   a. Cool and dry.
   b. Hot and humid.
   c. Warm and dry.

2. What's the highest temperature in Philadelphia in five years?
   a. 108 °F.
   b. 100 °F.
   c. 30 °C.

3. How many people died as the result of the weather last month in California?
   a. Over 140.
   b. Over 150.
   c. Over 145.

4. What's the temperature in Bismarck, North Dakota on Sunday?
   a. 38 °C.
   b. 44 °C.
   c. 112 °C.

IV. Listen and fill in the following blanks.

1. This week some parts of US are ______________________________ rising heat and humidity levels.
2. Many parts have ____________________ some of the highest temperatures in years.
3. As the heat is expected to slowly edge further east, the New York Mayor has already ____ in anticipation of the extreme heat.
4. New York, Washington, and Baltimore are all expecting __________________________ ___________ before the heat subsides again on Thursday.
5. In Minneapolis the temperatures ____________________ to over 100 degrees Fahrenheit (38°C) for the first time in over a decade.
6. Bismarck had temperatures of 100°F or higher for eight days ____________________.

Text Two

I. Words and expressions

monsoon /mɒn'su:n/ *n.* 季风，雨季
seasonal /'si:zənəl/ *adj.* 季节性的
subcontinent /ˌsʌb'kɒntɪnənt/ *n.* 次大陆
torrential /tɒ'renʃəl/ *adj.* 猛烈的
disrupt /dɪs'rʌpt/ *v.* 破坏，使中断
paddy /'pædɪ/ *n.* 稻谷
sugarcane /'ʃʊgəkeɪn/ *n.* 甘蔗
downpour /'daʊnpɔ:/ *n.* 倾盆大雨
recede /rɪ'si:d/ *v.* 后退
power line 电力线
Pakistan /ˌpɑ:kɪ'stɑ:n/ 巴基斯坦(南亚国家)
Bangladesh /ˌbɑ:ŋglə'deʃ/ 孟加拉国(南亚国家)
Indus /'ɪndəs/ 印度河(南亚)
Karachi /kə'rɑ:tʃɪ/ 卡拉奇(巴基斯坦南部港市)
Narmada /'nə:mədə/ 纳尔默达河(南亚)
Gujarat /ˌgu:dʒə'rɑ:t/ 古吉拉特邦(印度)
Maharashtra /ˌma:hə'rɑ:ʃtrə/ 马哈拉施特拉邦(印度)

II. Listen to confirm or to adjust

Listen and find out if your expectations are the same as or different from what you hear. If different, find the correct one or ones from ***Make your prediction****.*

III. Listen and choose the best answer to each of the following questions.

1. During which months does the southwest monsoon set in across the Indian subcontinent?
   a. June, July and August.
   b. June, July and September.
   c. June, July, August and September.
   d. June, August and September.

2. Which of the following is not common in the monsoon season?
   a. Rain.
   b. Drought.
   c. Flood.
   d. Wind.

3. What happened in western India?
   a. Many people were relocated.
   b. Around 25,000 people were killed.
   c. Some villages were reduced to rubbles.
   d. Water levels rose to a record high.

4. How many people died in India since monsoon set in?
   a. 25,000.
   b. 19.
   c. 48.
   d. 343.

IV. Listen and fill in the following blanks.

1. The southwest monsoon, which brings seasonal rains to Pakistan, India and Bangladesh, is now ____________________________ across the Indian subcontinent.
2. In Pakistan, several rivers were ____________________, including the Indus.
3. In the low-lying areas of western India, rivers ________________________________ and flooded large areas.
4. In neighbouring Maharashtra state water levels were ____________________________, but thousands were still moved to safer ground.

Part Three Look at This

了解气象新闻的特点　熟悉气象新闻中的术语

气象新闻大多报道某地区某段时间内异常的天气情况或灾难性气候，以及这些天气情况或灾难性气候给人类带来的不便和造成的损失乃至伤亡。因此听这类新闻时，我们关注的焦点应该是地点、时间、气候的异常情况及造成的后果等。有的英语学习者觉得气象新闻难懂，原因不外乎两点：生疏的地名和成串的术语。对此我们应该：

1. 调整期望值。有的英语学习者要求自己听懂并记住气象新闻中每个地方的天气情况，这种不切实际的期望会导致过度紧张和沮丧，使得我们不仅听不懂、记不住，而且一碰到气象新闻就心生恐惧，更加影响理解。试想我们听母语播报的气象新闻时也不可能背出每个地方的每种天气情况，所以听英语气象新闻只需达到通常理解的要求即可，刚开始时听不全亦无妨。

2. 平时在做听力练习之前浏览生词表或题目以熟悉相关地名，避免听时遇到满篇生词。听时焦点集中于地名、时间、气候的异常情况和由此造成的后果。有时报道中还会提到当地政府应对灾难性气候的措施，听这类新闻时也可以关注一下这方面的信息。

3. 掌握基本的气象术语对听懂气象新闻极为关键。下面我们归纳了一些常用的气象术语：

a. 温度（从低到高）
freezing, cold, chilly, cool, mild, warm, hot, scorching

b. 湿度（从小到大）
dry, damp, humid, wet, close, suffocating

c. 雨量（从小到大）
drizzle, light rain, shower, heavy rain, downpour

d. 风力（从小到大）
breeze, light wind, moderate wind, strong wind, storm

e. 云量（从少到多）
sunny, clear, cloudy, overcast

f. 恶劣天气及相关灾害
dense fog, smog, cold wave, heatwave, monsoon, hurricane, tornado, typhoon, twister, hail, blizzard, avalanche, tsunami, drought, flood

Part Four Here's More

Exercise One

Listen and choose the best answer to each of the following questions.

1. What's the weather like on 15 Aug 1952 in North Devon town of Camelford, Lynmouth?
   a. Rainy.
   b. Sunny.
   c. Cloudy.
   d. Foggy.

2. What disaster happened as a result of the weather?
   a. Drought.
   b. Flood.
   c. Smog.
   d. Fire.

3. How many people were killed in the disaster?
   a. 33.
   b. 34.
   c. 43.
   d. 44.

Exercise Two

Listen twice and complete the following summary with the key words.

From Jan 31st to Feb 1st, (1) ________, parts of East Anglia were (2) _________ by East Coast (3) __________. Over (4) ___________ people were killed and many more were made homeless. Over (5)__________ people were killed in continental Europe. As a result of high tides and a (6) ______________________, water was driven over the top of sea defences along the East Coast.

Exercise Three

Listen twice and complete the answers to the following questions.

1. What do you know about winter 1962–3?
   It's the _______________ winter since at least 1795.
2. What's the weather like on Feb 6–7, 1963?

It ______________ continuously for 36 hours.

3. What's the average temperature during the winter?

   It's only ______________.

4. How many people were killed by the direct effects of the severe weather?

   At least ______________ people.

Exercise Four

Listen and choose the best answer to each of the following questions.

1. How many named tropical storms have formed so far since the Atlantic hurricane season began on June 1st?
   a. One.
   b. Two.
   c. Three.
   d. Four.

2. How fast is the wind as a hurricane force?
   a. Up to 60 mph.
   b. Over 60 mph.
   c. Up to 74 mph.
   d. Over 74 mph.

3. In which direction is Chris expected to go?
   a. West-northwesterly.
   b. North.
   c. East-northwesterly.
   d. South.

Exercise Five

Listen twice and decide whether the following statements are true (T) or false (F).

1. Britain suffered a severe drought in 1976. ***T*** ☐ ***F*** ☐
2. There was continuous rain for between 35 and 42 days in southern England. ***T*** ☐ ***F*** ☐
3. Many people were forced to collect water from standpipes in the street in many parts of England and Wales. ***T*** ☐ ***F*** ☐
4. Drought Bill allowed local authorities to fine those who wasted water. ***T*** ☐ ***F*** ☐

Unit 16

Accidents and Catastrophes

Part One Before You Listen

I. Think and answer

1. What qualities are necessary when one handles an accident? What should you do in an emergency?
2. What emergency services should we turn to in case of an accident?
3. What can mankind do to deal with difficulties or even disasters brought about by forces of nature?
4. Do you think mankind can conquer nature? How can mankind cope with nature and live in harmony with her?

II. Make your prediction

Browse through all the information offered in this unit and predict the main idea of Text One and Text Two by choosing from a, b, c and d. You may choose more than one answer to indicate your prediction.

Text One

a. Rescue efforts to a bus-train collision.
b. A bus-train collision and the cause of the accident.
c. Victims of a bus-train collision.
d. Death toll of a bus-train collision.

Text Two

a. Reasons for a helicopter crash.

b. Living conditions of the victims after an earthquake.
c. The succeeding rescue efforts hampered after a severe earthquake.
d. A helicopter crash.

Part Two Listen Now

Text One

I. Words and expressions

swerve /swɜːv/ *v.* 突然转向
partially /ˈpɑːʃəlɪ/ *adv.* 不完全地，部分地
collision /kəˈlɪʒən/ *n.* 碰撞，冲突
negligence /ˈneglɪdʒəns/ *n.* 疏忽，粗心大意
death toll 死亡人数

II. Listen to confirm or to adjust

*Listen and find out if your expectations are the same as or different from what you hear. If different, find the correct one or ones from **Make your prediction**.*

III. Listen and complete the following table.

Type of accident	A bus-train collision.
Place	1. ________________, Colombo.
Cause	2. ________________.
Number of people killed	3. ________________.
Destination of the train	4. ________________ of Kandy.
Destination of the bus	5. ________________, Colombo.

IV. Listen and answer the following questions.

1. What was the bus doing when the accident happened?

   ____

2. What happened to the bus after it was hit and dragged by the train?

   ____

3. Was the train driver responsible for the accident?

   ____

4. Were there victims on the train?

   ____

Text Two

I. Words and expressions

devastating /ˈdevəsteɪtɪŋ/ *adj.* 破坏性很大的，毁灭性的
magnitude /ˈmægnɪtjuːd/ *n.* 巨大；重要性；(地震的)震级
hamper /ˈhæmpə/ *v.* 阻碍，妨碍；牵制
aftershock /ˈɑːftəʃɒk/ *n.* (地震的)余震
rubble /ˈrʌbl/ *n.* 瓦砾，(一堆)碎砖，碎石
geological /ˌdʒɪəʊˈlɒdʒɪkəl/ *adj.* 地质的
epicenter /ˈepɪsentə/ *n.* (地震的)震中
veranda /vəˈrændə/ *n.* 游廊，走廊
traumatic /trɔːˈmætɪk/ *adj.* 令人痛苦难忘的，造成精神创伤的
facility /fəˈsɪlətɪ/ *n.* (提供方便、服务等的)设施
shatter /ˈʃætə/ *v.* (使)粉碎，破碎
repatriate /riːˈpætrɪeɪt/ *v.* 遣返(某人)回国
drape /dreɪp/ *v.* 披，盖
coffin /ˈkɒfɪn/ *n.* 灵柩，棺材
condolence /kənˈdəʊləns/ *n.* 吊唁，哀悼，慰问的词句

II. Listen to confirm or to adjust

*Listen and find out if your expectations are the same as or different from what you hear. If different, find the correct one or ones from **Make your prediction**.*

III. Listen and complete the following table.

Type of disaster	An earthquake.
Place	1. ________________.
Magnitude	2. ________________.
Number of people killed	3. ________________.
Number of people injured	Not known.
Number of aftershocks	4. ________________.

IV. Listen and fill in the following blanks.

1. Efforts to get help to those earthquake victims have been hampered by ______________, ______________ and ______________ ________.
2. Ships carrying food and water are getting through, but ______________ and ______________ are holding up distribution.
3. An Australian military helicopter crashed, killing __________ men and __________ women of its __________ crewmembers.
4. Indonesian President says those killed in the helicopter crash will be awarded ______ ______________________________.

Part Three Look at This

事故或灾难类新闻的焦点

我们在听事故或灾难类新闻报道时，应该特别关注第一句句子，因为它往往涵盖了这样的信息：事故或灾难的类型、发生的地点和时间、伤亡人数或造成的损失。请看以下两条新闻报道的首句句子：

1. Unidentified gunmen had attacked the headquarters of the presidential guard in Tajikistan, killing thirteen guards.
2. The Mexican government says the first cases of cholera have been reported

following the hurricane which struck parts of the Pacific coast last week.

所以我们只要抓住了第一句，就抓住了事故或灾难类新闻报道的概要。

这类报道接下来会比较详细地讲述事故或灾难的过程、死亡人数、造成的损失以及营救措施等。如果是人为的事故，报道会提及原因。所以我们如果抓不住第一句，还可以从接下来的报道中获取信息。

总而言之，听事故或灾难类新闻报道时我们关注的焦点是：事故或灾难的类型、时间、地点、伤亡人数或损失、事故的原因等。

另外，这类新闻报道所使用的基本词汇是稳定的，要听懂事故或灾难类新闻，我们应该掌握一些描述事故和灾难的词汇。以下我们就这些词汇作一个归纳。

1. 关于事故

airplane crash（空难）；bus crash（撞车）；train crash（火车撞车）；collision（撞车）；collide（相撞）；derailment（出轨）；ship sink（沉船）；wreckage（残骸）；survivor（幸存者）；trapped passenger（被困乘客）；death toll（死亡人数）；fatality rate（伤亡率）；under investigation（在调查中）；emergency service（紧急服务）；emergency treatment（紧急治疗）；firedamp explosion（瓦斯爆炸）；terrorist activities（恐怖活动）；suicide bombing（自杀性爆炸）；shoulder-fired missile attacks（肩扛式地对空导弹袭击）；mass shootings（大范围射击）；deployments of chemical, biological, or radiological weapons（化学、生物、放射性武器的部署）

2. 关于灾难

earthquake（地震）；aftershock（余震）；epicenter（震中）；Richter scale（里氏震级）；seismic zone（地震带）；typhoon（台风）；hurricane（飓风）；cyclone（旋风，热带风暴）；blizzard（暴风雪，雪暴）；tornado（龙卷风）；monsoon（季风）；tsunami/tidal wave（海啸）；flood（水灾）；drought（干旱）；volcano eruption（火山爆发）；sandstorm（沙尘暴）；windstorm（风暴）；landslide（山崩）；mudslide/debris flow（泥石流）；avalanche（雪崩）；forest fire（森林火灾）；famine（饥荒）；evacuation（疏散）；widespread urban search and rescue（大范围市区搜寻和救援）

熟悉了这些词汇，听到事故或灾难类新闻时就不会感到陌生，而能够比较快地判断出播音员报道的是什么内容。

Part Four Here's More

You are going to hear two news reports of disasters. Listen and complete the following tables.

Exercise One

Type of disaster	1. ______________________.
Time	2. ______________________.
Place	3. ______________________.
Magnitude	4. ______________________.
Number of people confirmed dead	5. ______________________.
Number of people injured	6. ______________________.

Exercise Two

Type of disaster	1. ______________________.
Speed	2. Up to ______________________.
Time	3. ______________________.
Place	4. Coastal towns in ______________________.
Estimated deaths	5. ______________________.
Destruction	6. ____________ were destroyed, ____________ were downed, and ____________ sank.
Rescue work	7. A search continues, ______________________.

Unit 17

Big Churches, Big Crowds

Part One Before You Listen

I. Think and answer

1. Have you heard of the Lakewood Church and Joel Osteen?
2. How do you appreciate the notion that for churches, the bigger, the better?
3. Do you think churches should focus on a particular group of people or should be open to people of all walks of life?

II. Make your prediction

Browse through all the information offered in this unit and predict the main idea of Text One and Text Two by choosing from a, b, c and d. You may choose more than one answer to indicate your prediction.

Text One

a. The Lakewood Church is growing big.
b. Pastor Joel Osteen is growing popular.
c. The Lakewood Church is not doing well.
d. Pastor Joel Osteen is being criticized.

Text Two

a. Opposing views of the megachurch trend.
b. Different approaches to Christianity.
c. The diversity of the Lakewood Church.
d. The building of the Lakewood Church.

Part Two Listen Now

Text One

I. Words and expressions

spirituality /ˌspɪrɪtjʊ'ælətɪ/ *n.* 灵性
resemble /rɪ'zembl/ *v.* 与……相似
orchestra /'ɔːkɪstrə/ *n.* 管弦乐队
choir /'kwaɪə/ *n.* 合唱团；唱诗班
lyrics /'lɪrɪks/ *n.* 歌词
overhead /'əʊvəhed/ *adj.* 在头顶上的
pastor /'pɑːstə/ *n.* 本堂牧师
crane /kreɪn/ *n.* 摄像机升降机架
congregation /ˌkɒŋgrɪ'geɪʃən/ *n.* 教堂会众
ministry /'mɪnɪstrɪ/ *n.* 布道
oversee /ˌəʊvə'siː/ *v.* 监督
remodel /ˌriː'mɒdəl/ *v.* 改造
freeway /'friːweɪ/ *n.* 高速公路
Compaq 康柏(公司名)

II. Listen to confirm or to adjust

*Listen and find out if your expectations are the same as or different from what you hear. If different, find the correct one or ones from **Make your prediction**.*

III. Listen and complete the following table.

Profile of Joel Osteen	
Name	Joel Osteen.
Age	(1) ______________.

Occupation	Pastor.
Number of the registered members of his church in Houston	(2) ____________.
Title of his best-selling book	*Your Best Life Now — Seven steps to Living at Your Full Potential.*
Number of copies of the book sold	(3) ____________.
Current project	Overseeing the (4) ____________of the former Compaq Center sports arena as a new place for his weekly service.

IV. Listen and fill in the following blanks.

1. There is __________________ in the spirituality at the Lakewood Church.
2. Services here sometimes ______________ a rock concert or theatrical event.
3. The music is provided by a 10-piece orchestra and an onstage choir, with ______________ ___________ joining in, reading the lyrics from overhead television screens.
4. Close-up images of Pastor Joel Osteen and others are provided by cameras on cranes and platforms placed ______________________________.
5. The above description of the church leaves people the impression that the church service is ________________________________ (huge/small, lively/boring, dynamic/static).

Text Two

I. Words and expressions

critic /ˈkrɪtɪk/ *n.* 批评家
venue /ˈvenjuː/ *n.* 地点
charity /ˈtʃærətɪ/ *n.* 慈善
megachurch /ˈmegətʃɜːtʃ/ *n.* 超级教堂
civic /ˈsɪvɪk/ *adj.* 市民的
auditorium /ˌɔːdɪˈtɔːrɪəm/ *n.* 礼堂
sanctuary /ˈsæŋktjʊərɪ/ *n.* 圣所

ethnic /ˈeθnɪk/ *adj.* 种族的
diversity /daɪˈvɜːsətɪ/ *n.* 多样性
water down 掺水冲淡

II. Listen to confirm or to adjust

Listen and find out if your expectations are the same as or different from what you hear. If different, find the correct one or ones from ***Make your prediction****.*

III. Listen and decide whether the following statements are true (T) or false (F).

1. Critics of the Osteen approach to Christianity think that the investment in the new venue is rather wasteful and unwise. *T* ☐ *F* ☐
2. Some more traditional Christian leaders think the idea of megachurch trend has diluted Christianity. *T* ☐ *F* ☐
3. William Martin is also opposed to Joel Osteen's approach to Christianity. *T* ☐ *F* ☐
4. The large buildings of churches nowadays seem to attract all kinds of people. *T* ☐ *F* ☐
5. Lakewood's success can be partly attributed to its openness to people of all kinds. *T* ☐ *F* ☐

IV. Listen and complete the answer to the following question.

Question: In what sense can we say a remarkable thing about the Lakewood Church is its diversity?

Answer:

1. Lakewood church's success has to do with its openness to people from ________________ ____.
2. There are ________________ people who attend services each week, and it is approximately a third, a third, a third — ________________, ________________, and ________________ — with some ____________ as well, a growing number.
3. Joel Osteen believes that when you have a message to help people and you are sincere, it does not matter ________________________ or ____________________________ you are.

Part Three Look at This

新闻特写中的描写

英语学习者在听新闻特写时往往会感到困难，这是因为与惜字如金的时事新闻不同，新闻特写有其自身的特点。本课要讲的是新闻特写里的描写，它可以出现在新闻的开头，也可以出现在当中，甚至末尾，使得整则新闻特写颇有文学味道，同时自然也增加了理解的难度。

那么，我们应该如何应对新闻特写中的文学性描写呢？关键是要理解精义，而不要花费太多精力咀嚼描写中的修辞。例如 Text One 的开头就是一大段描写：

> There is plenty of spirit in the spirituality at the Lakewood Church. Services here sometimes resemble a rock concert or theatrical event. The music is provided by a 10-piece orchestra and an onstage choir, with church-goers joining in, reading the lyrics from overhead television screens. Close-up images of Pastor Joel Osteen and others are provided by cameras on cranes and platforms placed in and around the congregation.

游刃有余的听力高手听到这段描写可以在脑海中形成一幅相应的生动画面，但是一般的听众可能会听得云里雾里，不知所云。其实这段文字和其他体裁的英语材料有个共同点，即开头是一个话题句，接下来的文字是围绕 There is plenty of spirit in the spirituality at the Lakewood Church 这句话题句而展开的。所以，我们首先应该抓住话题句，然后找出其余的内容是从哪几个方面展开的。在上述段落里，如果无法理解第一句话的意思，那么第二句 Services sometimes resemble a rock concert or theatrical event 是对前句的注释。而接下来的两句话则是通过对 music 和 images of the pastor and others 的叙述来展开第二句。

我们听新闻很大程度上是想了解发生了什么，换言之，我们关注的是事实。所以我们在听新闻特写时可以抓住关键词，听出实质性的信息。听懂开始的几句话很重要，然后抓住围绕话题句展开的细节。建议特别关注听到的名词，如 Lakewood Church，services，rock concert，music，church-goers，images，pastor，cameras 等，并关注它们之间的关系。这样我们就可以大致把握整段描写的意思，即 The service in the Lakewood Church is as lively as a rock concert, with music from the choir and church-goers, as well as images of the pastor and others on big screens。

Part Four Here's More

Exercise One

Listen twice and fill in the blanks, then answer the question that follows.

It's a seemingly (1) ____________ stream of (2) ____________, as the faithful file passed (3) ____________. Outside is a sea of humanity, stretching (4) ____________ down the road that leads to the Vatican.

They wait, sometimes for (5) ____________, often breaking into song, or shouting the pope's name and applauding. According to the Vatican, (6) ____________ people pass through the doors of Saint Peter's (7) ____________. The crowds have been calm, but they keep coming, and their sheer numbers have already presented (8) ____________ for the city of Rome.

Question: What is the major message that you can learn from the above description?

____

____

Exercise Two

Listen twice and fill in the blanks, then answer the question that follows.

As (1) ____________ displays ushered in (2) ____________ from Paris to Athens, Rome to Madrid, curiosity drove Europeans to cash machines at (3) ____________ for the first look at the brightly colored (4) ____________.

Question: What can you mainly learn from the above description?

____

____.

Unit 18

Golden Globe Awards

Part One Before You Listen

I. Think and answer

1. What kind of movie (e.g. comedy, horror movie, thriller, etc.) is your favorite?
2. Which do you prefer, the Western movies or the Chinese ones? And why?
3. Who is your favorite actor/actress/director?
4. Usually how do you decide on a movie to watch? For example, by the plot, the actor or other factors?

II. Make your prediction

Browse through all the information offered in this unit and predict the main idea of Text One and Text Two by choosing from a, b, c and d. You may choose more than one answer to indicate your prediction.

Text One

a. Some Golden Globe awards have been announced and given out at the annual Hollywood ceremony.

b. *The Aviator* is a movie about a billionaire and flight pioneer.

c. Winners made speeches after they had been awarded prizes.

d. Clint Eastwood thanked the actor and actress at the ceremony.

Text Two

a. More awards were announced and given out, and their winners' speeches were delivered at the ceremony.

b. Foxx was very thankful to Ray Charles when he won the award.

c. Many actors expressed their thanks when giving a message.

d. Robin Williams was awarded a great honor by the Golden Globe Awards.

Part Two Listen Now

Text One

I. Words and expressions

aviator /ˈeɪvɪeɪtə/ *n.* 飞行者
indicator /ˈɪndɪkeɪtə/ *n.* 指示物
prestigious /preˈstɪdʒəs/ *adj.* 有声望的
eccentric /ɪkˈsentrɪk/ *adj.* 古怪的 *n.* 怪人
portrayal /pɔːˈtreɪəl/ *n.* 描绘，描写
complimentary /ˌkɒmplɪˈmentərɪ/ *adj.* 赞美的
capricious /kəˈprɪʃəs/ *adj.* 突发奇想的，反复无常的
playboy /ˈpleɪbɔɪ/ *n.* 花花公子
privileged /ˈprɪvɪlɪdʒd/ *adj.* 有特殊荣幸的
pinnacle /ˈpɪnəkl/ *n.* 尖峰，顶点
veteran /ˈvetərən/ *adj.* 经验丰富的
dramatic /drəˈmætɪk/ *adj.* 戏剧类的
Best Motion Picture-Drama 最佳剧情片
Best Musical or Comedy 最佳音乐片 / 喜剧片
starring role 主角
the Golden Globe Awards 美国电影金球奖

II. Listen to confirm or to adjust

Listen and find out if your expectations are the same as or different from what you hear. If different, find the correct one or ones from ***Make your prediction****.*

III. Listen and choose the best answer to each question you hear.

1. a. On Sunday in Hollywood.
   b. On Saturday in Hollywood.
   c. On Sunday in Washington.
   d. On Sunday in Hollywood Foreign Press Association.

2. a. One.
   b. Two.
   c. Three.
   d. Four.

3. a. The Hollywood Foreign Press Association.
   b. The director of *The Aviator*.
   c. The greatest contributor to the movie world.
   d. His parents.

4. a. Best Drama.
   b. Best Dramatic Actor.
   c. Best Musical or Comedy.
   d. Best Dramatic Actress.

5. a. *The Aviator*.
   b. *Sideways*.
   c. *Million Dollar Baby*.
   d. *Closer*.

IV. Listen and fill in the following blanks.

1. Since held about ____________________ earlier than the Oscar Awards, the Golden Globe Awards is regarded as the ______________ of it.
2. ______________________ relates the story of an eccentric billionaire and ____________ __________ — Howard Hughes. Due to his excellent ______________ of this character, Leonardo DiCaprio was named ____________________________.
3. As the director of *Million Dollar Baby*, Clint Eastwood also played ______________ _______ in the movie and was fortunately named ____________________. In his speech, he was very thankful to Morgan Freeman as well as Hilary Swank who won an award too for her _____________________ in the movie.

Text Two

I. Words and expressions

biography /baɪ'ɒgrəfɪ/ *n.* 传记
infidelity /ˌɪnfɪ'delətɪ/ *n.* 背叛，不忠诚
comedian /kə'miːdjən/ *n.* 喜剧演员
egotistical /ˌɪːgə'tɪstɪkəl/ *adj.* 自负的，自大的
affair /ə'feə/ *n.* 风流韵事
star /stɑː/ *v.* 使担任主角
seaman /'siːmən/ *n.* 海员，水手
quadriplegic /ˌkwɒdrɪ'pledʒɪk/ *adj.* 四肢麻痹的，四肢瘫痪的
rhythm and blues 节奏布鲁斯（一种音乐类型）
supporting role 配角

II. Listen to confirm or to adjust

Listen and find out if your expectations are the same as or different from what you hear. If different, find the correct one or ones from ***Make your prediction****.*

III. Listen and answer the following questions.

1. What was Ray Charles and at what age did he die?

____

2. What did Ray Charles compare life to?

____

3. What award did Annette Bening receive?

____

4. What award did Robin Williams receive?

____

5. How did Robin Williams express his thanks?

____

IV. Listen and complete the following table.

The Awarded Movies

Name of the movie	The award	The plot
Ray	(1) ______________.	A film biography of Ray Charles.
Closer	(2) ___________ Actor and Actress.	A story of (3)__________ who learn the consequences of (4) __________.
The Sea Inside	(5) ______________.	A true story of a (6) ________ who is unable to move his legs or arms and fights for (7) _____ years for (8) ________.

Part Three Look at This

颁奖类新闻报道的结构及典型句型

听新闻时，我们常常会听到各类颁奖报道。此类新闻报道信息量大，要报道一个系列里的各种奖项，所以涉及面比较广。这类新闻报道有一些特点：首先，信息与信息之间很少有必然联系，往往直接从一个奖项转到下一个奖项，很少有过渡。其次，从本单元的颁奖新闻报道中我们可以发现，紧接着每一部提到的影片名字，都有对该影片内容的简短介绍。最后，在揭晓奖项之后，往往会插播一段得奖人的致词(message)，或者一段影片音像资料(如本单元听力材料中插播了部分电影的片断)。除此之外，在报道得奖影片及获奖人时常采用典型句型，大致可以总结为如下几种：

1. (the name of a prize/award) goes to (a person's name)
2. (a person' name) received (the name of a prize/award)
3. (a person's name) was awarded (the name of a prize/award)
4. (a person's name) was named (the name of a prize/award)
5. (a person's name) won (the name of a prize/award)
6. (a person's name) took home (the name of a prize/award)

除了了解颁奖类新闻报道的特点以外，了解一些和电影有关的词汇，对提高英语娱乐新闻的听力理解也很有帮助。以下我们对这类词汇作个小小的总结：

1. 电影的不同类型(genre)

action(动作片); adventure(冒险片); animation(动画片); comedy(喜剧片); crime(犯罪片); drama(剧情片); family film(家庭片); fantasy(幻想片); horror(恐怖

片)；mystery(侦探片)；romance(爱情片)；sci-fi(科幻片)；thriller(惊悚片)；western(西部片)；musical(音乐片 / 歌舞片)；documentary(纪录片)

2. 电影工作者

star/lead(主角)；support(配角)；stand-in(替身演员)；stunt man/woman(特技替身演员)；extra/walk-on(临时演员)；playwright(编剧)；adapter(改编)；producer(制片人)；cameraman/set photographer(摄影师)；assistant cameraman(摄影助理)；set decorator(布景师)；makeup artist(化妆师)；lighting engineer(灯光师)；film editor(剪辑师)；sound engineer/recording director(录音师)；script holder(场记)

3. 其他

blockbuster(轰动一时的大片)；behind the scene(幕后)；billing(演员表)；box office(票房)；buzz(口碑)；film shooting(电影拍摄)；shot(镜头)；footage(连续镜头)；A-certificate (A 级[儿童不宜])；B movie(B 级片)；premiere(首映)；release([影片]发行)；shoot(拍摄)；scene/set(场景 / 布景)；screenplay(电影剧本)；adaptation(改编)；camera(摄影机)；subtitles(字幕)；sound recording(录音)；dubbing(配音)；projection booth(放映室)；motion picture/film studio(电影制片厂)；filmdom(电影界)

当然电影方面的词汇远不止这些，所以我们在日常学习中还要不断地积累相关知识。

Part Four Here's More

Exercise One

You will hear a piece of news about National Book Awards of the US. Listen carefully and complete the following table.

Award	Winner	Works	Message
The (1) ________ ______ Award.	Robert Caro.	*Master of the Senate: The Years of Lyndon Johnson.*	I'm really lucky to (2) ____________ ____________ and trying to untangle (理顺) and understand the manipulations (手法) and devices by which Lyndon Johnson acquired and used, for good and for ill, (3) ____________ ____________.

The Fiction Award.	Julia Glass.	(4) ______________. The book (5) ______ ________________ in the lives of a Scottish family.	... a book can be a sailing vessel, (6) ___ ______________, a tree house, a fabulous (7) _____________ ____, the wise, crusty grandmother you lost when you were too young to need her to be around you.
The (8) _______ ______________ Literature Award.	(9) __________.	*The House of the Scorpion*. The story tells about a clone struggling to (10) ___________ ________________.	

Exercise Two

You will hear some job descriptions about filmmaking. Listen carefully and fill in the following blanks.

1. ________ are those who ______________________, especially instead of ______________________________________.
2. __________ create ___________ and tell stories through _______________.
3. ____________ keeps a detailed record of progress when ________________.
4. ________ is involved throughout _______________________ from inception to completion, including coordination, supervision and control of all other talents and crafts.
5. ________ has the challenging task of bringing together the many complex pieces of _______ — the ____ — into a unified whole.
6. ________________ take ____________ on a ____________ and select which _______________________ to use, and then cut them together to form a cohesive and interesting story.

Unit 19

Cutting Back on Smoking in Movies

Part One Before You Listen

I. Think and answer

1. What do you know about Hollywood?
2. Is watching movies an important entertainment in your life?
3. Do you agree that some images in movies can affect a person's real-life behavior? If so, can you give some examples?
4. It's not rare to see smoking images in movies. Is it good? If not, what would you suggest we do with it?

II. Make your prediction

Browse through all the information offered in this unit and predict the main idea of Text One and Text Two by choosing from a, b, c and d. You may choose more than one answer to indicate your prediction.

Text One

a. Many young people love movies with smoking images, which poses a worrying problem.
b. Hollywood moviemakers ignore the issue of smoking movies.
c. Dr. Fielding and Professor Glantz appeal for cutting back on smoking in movies.
d. Now smoking in public places is eliminated in more and more American cities.

Text Two

a. A growing number of people around the world are taking action to resist smoking in movies.

b. Professor Glantz gives some suggestions to warn viewers against smoking.

c. Professor Glantz argues that there is a link between smoking and movies, and smoking movies actually advertise for tobacco companies.

d. Hollywood moviemakers argue against Professor Glantz.

Part Two Listen Now

Text One

I. Words and expressions

live-action /ˈlaɪvækʃən/ *adj.* (影片)实景真人摄制的
portray /pɔːˈtreɪ/ *v.* 描绘，描写
perplexing /pəˈpleksɪŋ/ *adj.* 使人困惑的，令人费解的
proactive /prəʊˈæktɪv/ *adj.* 主动的
glamour /ˈglæmə/ *n.* 魅力；魔法；迷人的美
behind-the-scenes /bɪˈhaɪndðəˈsiːnz/ *adj.* 幕后的
breast cancer 乳腺癌

II. Listen to confirm or to adjust

Listen and find out if your expectations are the same as or different from what you hear. If different, find the correct one or ones from ***Make your prediction***.

III. Listen and choose the best answer to complete each of the following statements.

1. ________ percent of the movies welcomed by young people have smoking images.
   a. 80
   b. 18
   c. More than 80
   d. 8

2. In Dr. Fielding's opinion, Hollywood hasn't been very helpful in the issues such as ________.
   a. AIDS
   b. breast cancer
   c. hunger

d. smoking

3. The so-called International Day of Action is ________.
   a. to celebrate the biggest day of the year in US movie calendar
   b. usually held after Oscar Sunday
   c. to appeal for restriction of smoking images in movies
   d. held on Feb 22 every year.

4. Professor Glantz describes the meetings he used to attend as ________.
   a. useless
   b. quiet
   c. behind-the-scenes
   d. All of the above.

IV. Listen and fill in the following blanks.

Dr. Jonathan Fielding: the (1) ______________________ director for Los Angeles County
His points:

- Most movies have smoking images and this surely makes young people more likely to (2) ______________________________.
- The entertainment industry shouldn't continue to (3) __________________________ ________________________, that is, to keep smoking out of movies, because it could (4) ____________________________ every year in the world.

Stan Glantz: a (5) ________________________ at the University of California, San Francisco
His points:

- Smoking in public places should be eliminated.
- (6) ____________________________ should be started in order to draw the public's attention to the issue of smoking in movies.

Text Two

I. Words and expressions

bristle /ˈbrɪsl/ *v.* 被激怒
censorship /ˈsensəʃɪp/ *n.* 审查制度
for one's part 就某人来说
Marlboro /ˈmɑːlbərə/ 万宝路(一种香烟品牌)
Senegal /ˌsenɪˈgɔːl/ 塞内加尔(西非国家)
Vietnam /ˌvjetˈnæm/ 越南(东南亚国家)

II. Listen to confirm or to adjust

*Listen and find out if your expectations are the same as or different from what you hear. If different, find the correct one or ones from **Make your prediction**.*

III. Listen and choose the best answer to each question you hear.

1. a. Coughing each time an actor lights a cigarette in the movie.
   b. Meeting with reporters to discuss the smoking issue.
   c. Complaining to moviemakers.
   d. Protesting the prominent display of a cigarette brand in movies.

2. a. The United States.
   b. Canada.
   c. Both the United States and Canada.
   d. The countries outside the United States and Canada.

3. a. The link between movies and real-life violence.
   b. The link between movies and smoking.
   c. The link between movies and other harmful behavior.
   d. All of the above.

IV. Listen and decide whether the following statements are true (T) or false (F).

1. Professor Glantz's organization, called Smokefree Movies Action Network, has helped organize protests and educational events outside the US and Canada. *T* ☐ *F* ☐
2. Professor Glantz suggests smoking should be kept out of youth-rated movies as well as adult-only movies. *T* ☐ *F* ☐
3. Cigarette companies have always been legally allowed to advertise their products in movies. *T* ☐ *F* ☐
4. Smoking images in movies are in fact a form of advertising for tobacco companies. *T* ☐ *F* ☐

V. Listen and fill in the following blanks.

1. The portrayal of smoking is advertising that people don't realize ________________ ________________________. And once people are made aware of it and thinking about it, then ________________________________ as well any more.

2. In some theaters in Canada, the tickets have ______________________________ printed on the back. In addition, on-screen notices before a movie begins can also ______________ ______________________________, and such ads are now being shown in New York State and Vermont.

Part Three Look at This

电影奥斯卡奖

每年2月，当美国电影艺术科学院(the Academy of Motion Picture Arts and Sciences)公布学院奖，即电影奥斯卡奖的候选名单(nomination list)时，全世界的奥斯卡迷们就开始翘首以待。一个月后，大约34 000个家庭会守在电视机旁，观看各个奖项到底会花落谁家。说起奥斯卡奖的历史，要追溯到美国电影艺术科学院成立的1927年。当时，学院组委会的任务之一就是要给那些优秀电影及电影人设立奖项，以推动电影产业的不断发展和电影质量的提高。从第一届奥斯卡颁奖典礼算起，已经有超过2 300个奥斯卡小金人(little golden statuette)被授予美国和其他地区杰出的电影人。而纵观奥斯卡的历史，也是趣事逸闻不断，比如早年的奥斯卡颁奖典礼对公众出售门票、有关"奥斯卡奖"名称来历的种种传说等等。

Part Four Here's More

Exercise

You will hear an introduction of the Academy Awards. While listening, do the following exercises.

I. Listen and choose the proper answers to the following question.

Which of the following points are included in this recording about the Academy Awards?

a. The origin of the Academy Awards.

b. The great change in the history of the Academy Awards.

c. Some interesting things in the history of the Academy Awards.

d. The description of the Oscar statuette.

e. The detailed introduction of several famous actors.

f. A popular story about the nickname — Oscar.

II. Listen and choose the best answer to each question you hear.

1. a. In 1927. b. In May 1928.
   c. In May 1929. d. In 1930.

2. a. 250. b. 10.
   c. 200. d. 50.

3. a. In 1931. b. In the late 1930's.
   c. After 1939. d. In 1939.

4. a. In Los Angles. b. In Hollywood.
   c. In Chicago. d. In New York.

5. a. *Titanic*. b. *Titanic* and *Ben-Hur*.
   c. *Ben-Hur*. d. Neither *Titanic* nor *Ben-Hur*.

6. a. Woody Allen. b. Katherine Hepburn.
   c. Jack Nicholson. d. None of the above.

III. Listen and fill in the following blanks.

1. At the first Academy Awards ceremony, some people might buy tickets to attend it. But today there are no tickets for ________________________. Without ________________, attendance is not allowed.
2. Margaret Herrick, ________________________, thought the statuette looked like her Uncle Oscar. After she said so, the Academy staff started to refer to it by this name.
3. The Oscar statuette is the figure of a knight, ______________________ and standing on a reel of film. The five spokes of the film reel signify ____________________________ of the Academy: actors, _______________, producers, ________________ and writers.

Unit 20

African-American Immigrants

Part One Before You Listen

I. Think and answer

1. Do you know why America is called a nation of immigrants?
2. Where is Houston in US?
3. What do you think of the idea of some new African immigrants about promoting their culture in the US?
4. Suppose you're an African immigrant, can you think out some effective ways to help the people of the US understand your culture?

II. Make your prediction

Browse through all the information offered in this unit and predict the main idea of Text One and Text Two by choosing from a, b, c and d. You may choose more than one answer to indicate your prediction.

Text One

a. African officials and oil industry executives often come to Houston.

b. Kenny owns a restaurant specializing in African food in Houston.

c. Some African immigrants in Houston are making every effort to build an identity for their culture and have their own place there.

d. Most people living in Houston now are from Nigeria.

Text Two

a. Generally, the people in the US have a good impression of Africa because of the positive reports.

b. Sam sells videos and DVDs of African movies so as to promote the understanding of Africa and Africans among the people in the US.

c. Nigeria is famous for the film production industry.

d. According to statistics, African immigration is relatively small and the majority of the African-born immigrants are living and working in Houston.

Text One

I. Words and expressions

trace /treɪs/ *v.* 追溯
clout /klaʊt/ *n.* 影响
cling to 紧紧依靠

II. Listen to confirm or to adjust

*Listen and find out if your expectations are the same as or different from what you hear. If different, find the correct one or ones from **Make your prediction**.*

III. Listen and choose the best answer to each question you hear.

1. a. In Nigeria.
   b. In Houston, the US.
   c. In the southeast of Houston.
   d. None of the above.

2. a. It clings to a certain area.
   b. It plays a large role in the society.
   c. It is popular among the people in the US.
   d. Americans are curious about it.

3. a. The African Group.
   b. The African Coalition.
   c. The African Immigrants.
   d. The African Cooperation.

4. a. People who understand African culture.
   b. Mostly African Americans who want to know more about their origins.
   c. People who are interested in African crafts and clothes.
   d. African Americans who want to go back to Africa.

IV. Listen and fill in the following blanks.

1. In order to make their culture ______________ and have their own place, many African immigrants in Houston are making their efforts. For example, Kenny runs an African restaurant to ________________________ for African food and culture. He has also formed a group with some other African immigrants, which aims to ____________________ ______________ of African immigrants in Houston and develop some influence both ________________________________.

2. By selling various African things in the stores, Sam — Kenny's friend — is trying to bring ____ to the people of the United States. However, he used to be __________________________ by some African Americans' ignorance of Africa.

Text Two

I. Words and expressions

depict /dɪˈpɪkt/ *v.* 描绘；描述
data /ˈdeɪtə/ *n.* (datum 的复数) 数据
Ghana /ˈgɑːnə/ 加纳 (西非国家)
Ethiopia /ˌiːθɪˈəʊpɪə/ 埃塞俄比亚 (东非国家)

II. Listen to confirm or to adjust

Listen and find out if your expectations are the same as or different from what you hear. If different, find the correct one or ones from ***Make your prediction****.*

III. Listen and answer the following questions.

1. What is frequently mentioned in news reports about Africa in the US?

____

2. How is Sam's business of selling African movie videos and DVDs?

____

3. How many people from Africa legally entered into the US in 2003?

____

4. Which African country has supplied the most immigrants to Houston?

____

IV. Listen and choose the proper answers to each of the following questions.

1. Which statements are true about the kind of movies Sam choose to sell?
   a. The stories in the movies are wonderful and the acting is great, too.
   b. The movie is unnecessarily in English but must interest Americans.
   c. The movies should not only entertain but also educate customers.
   d. Most of the movies come from Nigeria because there are many Nigerians in Houston.
   e. Sam is still looking for films from other African countries.
2. According to the news report, which statements are true about Houston?
   a. Most of the population in Houston is African immigrants.
   b. Many African immigrants come to Houston for work and study.
   c. Very likely Houston develops well in the oil and gas industry as well as higher education.
   d. Actually, around 27,000 African-born immigrants in the US are now living in Houston.
   e. There are much more Mexican immigrants than African immigrants working in Houston.

Part Three Look at This

美国的非洲裔移民

在17世纪初，最早来到弗吉尼亚(Virginia in the US)的大多数非洲移民并非出于自愿，而是作为奴隶被贩卖到美洲大陆，这也就注定了他们在随后的很长一段时间里处于社会的最底层。随着当时美国南方一些州(Virginia，Maryland，South Carolina等)种植园的大规模发展和对劳动力的迫切需求，奴隶制开始迅速发展并且合法化，于是众多非洲移民沦为奴隶，毫无人权，完全是奴隶主的私有财产，生活极其悲惨。然而不公正的制度并不能阻止非洲移民和他们的后代追求自由和权利，而他们的不懈努力最终不仅改变了美国，也改变了整个世界。现在在美国，除了大量老一代非洲移民的后代，每年还有源源不断的非洲国家的移民进入。仅在20世纪90年代，这个数字就达50多万，超过了过去150年间到美国的非洲移民的总数。纵观美国历史，杰出的非洲裔美国人众多，当代的有外交官Ralph Bunche、民权运动领袖Martin Luther King, Jr.、获诺贝尔文学奖的小说家Toni Morrison，还有最近的两任美国国务卿Colin Powell和Condoleezza Rice。总之，现在美国的非洲裔移民和他们的后代正在为非洲移民这个题目撰写着新的篇章。

Part Four Here's More

Exercise

I. Listen and choose the proper answers to the following question.

Which of the following are not included in the story about early African immigrants in North America?

a. The reason why they were willing to come to North America.
b. Their first settlement in North America.
c. The work they did.
d. Their sufferings in North America.
e. Their influencc on the world.

II. Listen and complete the following table.

Early African immigrants in North America	
The reason for their going to America	Most of them were brought to North America (1) ______________.
The first time they appeared for sale	In (2) ________.
The first place they appeared for sale	Virginia.

The things they did	They did almost every type of work, for example, — they (3) ____________________ and fruit orchards of New York and New Jersey; — they (4) ____________________ to mine iron and lead in the Ohio Valley; — they worked the docks in New England; — they (5) ____________________ in New York City; — they managed households from Florida to Maine, etc.
The contributions they have made	Their expertise shaped the industry and agriculture of this continent.
The sufferings they had	By (6) __________, the slavery system in colonial America was fully developed. It means slaves had (7) ____________________ to make decisions about their own lives and could be bought, sold, (8) ______________, rewarded, educated, or (9) ____________________.

III. *Listen and answer the following questions.*

1. What had African Americans battled for?

____

2. Now how many Americans claim African ancestry?

____

Appendix I
Listening Scripts

Unit 1
Childcare

Part Two Listen Now

Text One

VOICE ONE:

A half century ago, most mothers of young children in the United States did not work outside the home. But life has changed. The United States Census Bureau said that in two thousand two, sixty-four percent of mothers with a child under age six were in the workforce. If the father also works, the need for childcare is clear. The same is true if a parent is single.

VOICE TWO:

Sometimes grandparents or other family members watch over children. But most working parents must pay for care. And they often have to pay a lot. The Labor Department's Bureau of Labor Statistics says childcare costs for a full day begin at about four thousand dollars yearly. Many families pay ten thousand dollars yearly per child — and more.

The Urban Institute is an economic and social policy research organization. It reported in two thousand one about working families in America. The institute said nearly half of families with a child under thirteen spent about nine percent of their monthly earnings on childcare. The poorest families spent twenty-three percent.

VOICE ONE:

Some parents employ a person to supervise children in the parents' home. This person is often called a baby sitter or a nanny. Sometimes this care provider lives with the family.

Au pairs are foreign care providers. They live with families while supervising the families' children.

Some care providers open their own homes to one or more children. These, and other children's centers must meet the requirements of local and state governments. For example, a care provider can supervise only a limited number of children. The number depends on the children's ages. Care centers must show that they are protected against fires and other dangers. Yet once parents find a place, they cannot be sure they will stay. The care might not be as good as they hoped. Or the cost might increase. Or the parents might even be asked to take their son or daughter elsewhere if the child often bites or hits other children.

Text Two

VOICE ONE:

Head Start is the national preschool program for poor children. The goal is to prepare them for the educational system and life in general. But these programs cannot serve all needy children.

Getting good childcare that provides early education can be very difficult for poor families. The Census Bureau says there were thirty-seven million people in poverty in two thousand four. The poverty rate was twelve and seven-tenths percent, up two-tenths of one percent from the year before.

Now there are worries that money needed to rebuild areas hit by Hurricane Katrina could take away from early education and childcare.

VOICE TWO:

Parents often criticize the price of childcare. But daycare operators say many parents do not understand all the costs involved. These include food, drinks, toys, videos, games and crafts. They also include wages, taxes, insurance, transportation and things like cleaning supplies.

One person said on a childcare web site, "We providers are in this line of work for love of kids — not money!"

VOICE ONE:

Low pay is a major reason the industry has to replace many workers each year. Currently the lowest pay in the United States permitted under federal law is six dollars and seventy-five cents an hour.

The government says half of daycare workers earned less than seven dollars and eighteen cents an hour in two thousand two. Those employed in schools had median earnings of nine dollars and four cents per hour.

Pay depends on education. A caregiver who attended college earns more than a person who only finished high school. But the best pay is still not very high.

Part Four Here's More

Exercise One

Last week, in the United States, the Institute of International Education released its yearly report. "Open Doors Two Thousand Five" shows continued record growth in the number of American students who study in a foreign country.

The I.I.E. report says the number increased by almost ten percent in the two thousand three – two thousand four school year. This brought the number of Americans studying in another country to more than one hundred ninety-one thousand. The increase the year before was eight and one-half percent.

Interest in foreign study has increased for years. But I.I.E. officials say it has taken on greater importance since the terrorist attacks of September eleventh, two thousand one.

The newest report says sixty-one percent of the students went to Europe. But study in China increased by sixty-five percent. Study in Africa, the Middle East and Latin America, including Cuba, also increased.

The report says that while more Americans are studying abroad, they are staying for shorter periods of time. Six percent went for a full school year. Thirty-eight percent went for half a year. And fifty-six percent went for a shorter time.

The report says New York University has the largest number of students abroad. Michigan State University is second this year, followed by the University of California, Los Angeles.

Ten smaller schools each sent more than forty percent of their students abroad last year. The list includes Carleton College in Minnesota, Leon University in North Carolina and Lewis and Clark College in Oregon.

Exercise Two

Millions of American children between the ages of ten and fifteen attend middle schools. Middle school is the level between elementary and high school. Different middle schools have different numbers of grade levels. The first middle school opened in nineteen sixty.

The National Middle School Association is a group that advises and represents schools. One issue that concerns the group today is public school systems that are preparing to stop educating students in middle schools.

New York City is to close up to seventy-five percent of its middle schools. It plans to place those middle school students in either elementary schools or high schools.

Philadelphia, Pennsylvania, has already started to reduce its number of middle schools. Officials say the number will go from forty-six to eight by two thousand eight. They say students will learn more in their new schools than in the middle schools.

They say studies show that sixth graders in an elementary school perform better on tests than do sixth graders in a middle school.

They also note research showing that by the sixth grade, students show signs that they will or will not finish high school. These signs are low attendance, bad behavior, failing in mathematics and failing in English.

The officials say that placing sixth grade students in a middle school is not good for their learning or their future development.

Unit 2 Rags and Riches

Part Two Listen Now

Text One

I'm Steve Ember with the VOA Special English Development Report.

A new World Bank study says international migration helps reduce poverty in developing nations. At the same time, however, many countries that are small and poor lose highly skilled workers.

Migrants are people who move from place to place in search of work. The study shows that families with migrant workers in other countries have higher earnings than those without migrants.

Economists at the World Bank studied the effects of the money that migrant workers send to their families back home. Economist Maurice Schiff says the findings show that remittances reduce poverty and increase spending on education, health and investment.

The findings are based on information from families in three countries: Guatemala, Mexico and the Philippines. Mr. Schiff says further studies are being done in other countries.

The World Bank estimates that two hundred million people are migrants living outside their native country. It also estimates that about two hundred twenty-five thousand million dollars will be paid in remittances this year. In many countries, remittances supply more foreign exchange than anything else.

The study also found that migrant workers are more likely to move to a rich nation near their home country. Most migrants in Europe come from Africa and the Middle East. In the United States, migrant workers are generally from Mexico, Central America and Caribbean.

But international migration also means the problem of "brain drain." Many of the skilled workers needed to bring their countries out of poverty move to wealthier ones instead.

Text Two

I'm Steve Ember with In the News in VOA Special English.

This week, General Motors announced a three-year plan to lower its costs. The plan calls for GM to reduce its number of workers in North America by thirty thousand. That is a cut of seventeen percent. The company says it will close all or part of twelve factories in the United States and Canada.

Its chief executive officer, Rick Wagoner, says the cuts are necessary for the company to compete. General Motors has lost more than four thousand million dollars this year. And that is not its only problem. In October its largest supplier, Delphi, sought protection in bankruptcy court after heavy losses.

General Motors is the largest automobile maker in the world. But the company has struggled against foreign competitors, especially the Japanese automakers Toyota and Honda. Forty years ago, General Motors controlled half the market in the United States. Now it controls one-fourth of it.

GM will reduce production to better meet demand. It plans to produce just over four million cars and trucks a year in North America by the end of two thousand eight. That is thirty percent fewer than it built in two thousand two.

Industry experts blame the situation in part on poor decisions and vehicle designs that have not been very creative. Other reasons, they say, include costly health care and retirement payments.

The new cuts and measures announced earlier are expected to lower costs by about seven thousand million dollars next year.

The number of jobs to be lost, thirty thousand, is five thousand higher than Mister Wagoner had announced earlier this year. GM officials say they want to reduce employee numbers mainly through retirements.

Still, the United Auto Workers Union calls the cuts unfair. The labor union says it will do everything in its power to enforce job security programs.

Part Four Here's More

Exercise One

I'm Jim Tedder with the VOA Special English Health Report.

An international group says cases of measles in Africa have dropped by sixty percent since 1999. The group is known as the Measles Initiative. It says almost two hundred million children have been vaccinated against the disease in the past six years. The World Health Organization says vaccination campaigns in more than forty countries in Africa have saved one million children.

Exercise Two

I'm Faith Lapidus with the VOA Special English Development Report.

The World Future Society has published a special report about forces changing the world. The report is by Marvin Cetron, president of Forecasting International in Virginia, and Own Davies, a writer. It is called "Fifty-Three Trends Now Shaping the Future."

Exercise Three

A survey in the United States has indicated that just as many scientists believe in God today as 80 years ago, despite speculation that high levels of education would lead to more skepticism. The survey which was carried out by the University of Georgia used exactly the same questions as those in the original survey carried out by the psychologist James Luber in 1916. He found that 40% of scientists believed in God and in after-life. He predicted that the figure would drop with time, with better and more widespread education. But the results of the latest survey show that roughly the same proportion of today's scientists say they have a personal faith.

Unit 3 Health

Part Two Listen Now

Text One

American researchers have reported progress in learning how the ancient traditional Chinese method of acupuncture fights pain and other conditions. During acupuncture, very small, sharp needles are placed in the skin at targeted points on the body. Bruce Rosen presented an acupuncture study at a meeting of the American Psychosomatic Society in Orlando, Florida. Doctor Rosen is with the Harvard Medical School in Boston, Massachusetts.

Doctor Rosen reported that the study findings could show how the brain might help people suffering from a number of health problems. These include pain, unexplained worry and sadness and some disorders of the stomach and intestines. The findings also may aid people who are fighting dependence on substances like illegal drugs.

Doctor Rosen led a team that studied about twenty healthy people. The team examined the people with functional magnetic resonance imaging devices. MRI's can show changes in the flow of blood and the amount of oxygen in the blood. They studied the people before, during and after acupuncture. The researchers placed acupuncture needles in the skin on the people's hands. They chose places linked to pain relief in traditional Chinese acupuncture.

Most of the people reported that their hands felt heavy after the needles were placed. Blood flow to some areas of the brain decreased quickly in these people. Doctor Rosen said that was a sign that the acupuncture was working correctly.

But a few of the people said their hands hurt. Their needles were probably not placed correctly. Their MRI's showed an increase in blood in the same areas of the brain where the other people showed a decrease.

Doctor Rosen reported that this means that acupuncture eased the work of the brain. The affected brain areas are the forebrain, the cerebellum and the brainstem. They help control pain and emotions. These areas have a rich supply of a chemical called dopamine.

Doctor Rosen said the reduced blood flow may lead to changes in dopamine. This, in turn, leads to a reaction that releases endorphins. These brain chemicals reduce pain and help fight feelings of sadness.

Jerilyn Watson wrote this VOA Special English Health Report.

Text Two

American researchers say drinking tea may help strengthen the body's defense system against infection. Doctors at Brigham and Women's Hospital in Boston, Massachusetts, did the study.

The team studied a chemical found in black, green, oolong and pekoe tea. This chemical is an amino acid called L-theanine. The scientists say it may increase the strength of gamma delta T cells. That's the letter T, not the drink. Gamma delta T cells are part of the body's defenses.

First, the researchers mixed some of these cells with antigens found in the amino acid. Antigens help the body react to infection. Then the scientists added some bacteria. Within twenty-four hours, the cells produced a lot of interferon, a substance that fights infection. Cells not mixed with the antigens did not produce interferon.

In the second part of the study, eleven people drank five to six cups of black tea every day. Ten other people drank the same amount of instant coffee. That is dried coffee mixed with hot water. Two weeks later, and again two weeks after that, the researchers tested the blood of all twenty-one people. They also looked at what happened when they added bacteria to the blood cells. They found that the tea drinkers produced five times more interferon after they started drinking tea. The coffee drinkers did not produce interferon.

The findings appear in the *Proceedings of the National Academy of Sciences*. The National Institutes of Health and the Arthritis Foundation provided money for the research.

Doctor Jack Bukowski led the study. He says the antigens added to the gamma delta T cells were responsible for the increased reaction to the bacteria. He says the study also showed that the cells were able to remember the bacteria and fight them again the next time.

Earlier research already has found that tea can help prevent heart disease and cancer. Doctor Bukowski says the new study must be repeated with more people. If the findings are confirmed, he says, then tea drinking might also help protect against bacterial infections. He says the amino acid L-theanine could be removed from tea and used as a drug to strengthen the body's defenses.

This VOA Special English Health Report was written by Nancy Steinbach.

Part Four Here's More

Exercise

1. Sometimes people have the idea that all cholesterol in the blood is bad. But the body needs this fatty substance to create cells and hormones. The liver produces all the cholesterol we need.
2. US health officials say there is a new epidemic; it's called obesity. As diets higher in fat and sugar

become more widely available around the globe, fighting fat is not just a US problem.

3. One third of all the people in the world are infected with tuberculosis, or TB, a disease caused by bacteria in the lungs. Each year, eight million infected people become sick with the disease.
4. Very different viruses that spread through body waste or body fluids cause hepatitis. There are five forms of hepatitis, a vital disease that attacks the liver.
5. People who travel on long trips should know about a condition that can develop deep inside the legs. This condition is called deep vein thrombosis. A thrombosis is a blood clot, a condition where some blood thickens and blocks the flow.
6. Nicotine is the major substance in cigarettes that gives pleasure to smokers. Nicotine is a poison. The American Cancer Society says nicotine can kill a person when taken in large amounts.
7. Today, we tell about some emergency medical methods known commonly as first aid. First aid is the kind of medical care given to a victim of an accident or sudden sickness before trained medical help can arrive.
8. Alcohol affects the body's reaction to the hormone insulin. Insulin helps control sugar in the blood. And alcohol may improve how the body processes blood sugar.
9. There are drugs that doctors use to treat depression. But in developing countries, not many people are able to get these antidepressants.
10. A new study warns older people against taking growth hormone supplements to reverse the effects of aging. Human growth hormone is a natural substance important for normal growth and maintenance of tissues and organs.

Unit 4 Sharks

Part Two Listen Now

Text One

VOICE ONE:

This is Science in the News in VOA Special English. I'm Barbara Klein.

VOICE TWO:

And I'm Doug Johnson. On our program this week, we tell about sharks. They are among the oldest animals on Earth. Sharks are famous for attacking other sea creatures and even people. Yet they also have been threatened by human activities.

VOICE ONE:

Scientists say sharks have lived in the world's oceans for millions of years. Today, sharks live the same way they did more than two hundred million years ago, before dinosaurs existed on the Earth.

Scientists say there are more than three hundred fifty different kinds of sharks. Most sharks are about two meters long. The dogfish shark, however, is less than twenty centimeters in length. And the biggest whale shark can grow to a length of twenty meters.

Sharks do not have bones. The skeleton of a shark is made of cartilage. Human noses and ears are also made of cartilage.

VOICE TWO:

A shark has an extremely good sense of smell. It can find small amounts of substances in the water, such as blood, body liquids and chemicals produced by animals. Sharks also sense electrical and magnetic power linked to nerves and muscles of living animals. These powerful senses help them find their food. Sharks eat fish, other sharks, and plants that live in the ocean. Some sharks will eat just about anything. Many unusual things have been found in the stomachs of some tiger sharks. They include shoes, dogs, a cow's foot and metal protective clothing.

VOICE ONE:

Sharks grow slowly. Some kinds of sharks are not able to reproduce until they are twenty years old. Most reproduce only every two years. And they give birth to fewer than ten young sharks.

About forty percent of the different kinds of sharks lay eggs. The others give birth to live young. Some sharks carry their young inside their bodies, with a cord connecting the fetus to the mother, like humans do.

Text Two

VOICE ONE:

Scientists are beginning to understand the importance of sharks to humans. Medical researchers want to learn more about the shark's body defense system against disease. They know that sharks recover quickly from injuries.

Sharks appear never to suffer infections, cancer or heart diseases. Many people believe that shark cartilage can help prevent cancer. Scientists have questioned this idea. Yet they still study the shark in hopes of finding a way to fight human disease.

VOICE TWO:

Most sharks live in warm waters, but some can be found in very cold areas. Most sharks live in oceans. However, the bull shark leaves ocean waters to enter freshwater rivers and lakes. They have been found in the Zambezi River in Africa, the Mississippi River in the United States, and Lake Nicaragua in southwestern Nicaragua.

Sharks are important for the health of the world's oceans. They eat injured and diseased fish. Their hunting activities mean that the numbers of other fish in the ocean do not become too great. This protects the plants and other forms of life that exist in the oceans.

VOICE ONE:

People have long feared sharks because of their sharp teeth, aggressive actions and fame as fierce hunters. "Jaws" was the name of a popular book published in nineteen seventy-four. It told about people in an American coastal town who sought protection from a great white shark that killed swimmers in the ocean. Thirty years ago last month, the film version of the book was released. *Jaws* became one of the most popular American movies in history. The movie was extremely frightening.

However, experts say not all sharks are like the one shown in *Jaws*. Still, sharks attacked sixty-one people around the world last year. Twenty-seven of those attacks took place in North American waters. Twelve were in waters near the southeastern state of Florida.

Part Four Here's More

Exercise

The tundra is in the far northern parts of North America, Europe, and Asia. It is between the northern forests and the land where there is always snow. Most of the tundra land is flat.

Tundra is a Russian word that means "marshy plain." Except for the top few inches, the ground of a tundra is always frozen solid, and so the melted ice and snow cannot soak into the ground. They stay as ponds, lakes and marshes during the summer.

Tundras have very severe winters which last for about nine months of the year. The sun hardly shines at all in mid-winter. The weather is very cold. In some places it gets as cold as 90 degrees below zero. The ground often freezes as deep as 1,200 feet. There is some snow in the tundra, but the wind sweeps the snow away from the ground in many places.

No big trees grow in the tundra because the ground is frozen. There is not enough water for the roots. The plants in the tundra are small, and cling very close to the ground.

Summer in the tundra lasts from May to July. The sun shines day and night. During this time, the plants have to make enough food to last a whole year. In June the tundra is blanketed with gorgeous, blooming flowers. Plants grow almost everywhere.

About 900 different kinds of plants grow in the tundra. The most common ones are mosses, lichens, shrubs, wildflowers, and grasses. Perhaps the most important tundra plant is lichen, which can grow all year round. In the winter, lichen is the only food available for some animals.

Many animals live in the tundra. Even during the coldest winters, there are the Arctic fox, the snowshoe hare, the polar bear, the musk ox, and the ptarmigan, a bird that even has feathers on its feet to keep it warm.

The large musk oxen roam the tundra in herds. They have very thick coats of fur to keep them warm during the winter. A musk ox find plants to eat even under a layer of snow. The largest and strongest animal in the tundra is the polar bear. It usually finds a warm den and hibernates for most of the winter.

In the summer, the tundra is very busy with animal life. Many animals that left the tundra during the winter return from the warmer places. Herds of reindeer and caribou return from forests farther south where they spent the winter. Many birds, such as ducks, Canadian geese, and swans, come to spend the summer in the many lakes and ponds of the tundra. Many insects live around the water and fly among the flowers during the short tundra summer.

Unit 5 History of Jazz

Part Two Listen Now

Text One

ANNOUNCER:

Welcome to This Is America in VOA Special English. I'm Faith Lapidus.

In two thousand one, public television aired a series that told the story of jazz. Filmmaker and writer Ken Burns and writer Geoffrey Ward told how this music developed over the years. They showed how African-Americans created new sounds from their memories of slavery in the South. The filmmakers told how black, Creole and white Americans created a new musical form.

Today on This Is America, Shirley Griffith and Steve Ember present the first of two reports about the history of jazz.

VOICE ONE:

"Jazz" can mean different kinds of music: swing, bebop or fusion. Jazz can make the listener feel sad or joyful, quiet or full of energy. It can sound hot — or very cool.

Performers of jazz create some of the music as they play. They add their own notes to music that is written down. Each time a jazz musician plays a piece, it can sound fresh and new. Jazz musicians surprise listeners by breaking up traditional rhythms. And, they give greater intensity to unexpected parts of the music.

VOICE TWO:

Jazz probably had its roots in the nineteenth century. In the late eighteen-eighties, African-Americans began to develop new forms of music. They created blues music from the gospel music and sad songs of their years in slavery.

Ragtime also influenced the creation of jazz. This music first gained popularity in the eighteen-nineties in the South. African-American piano player Scott Joplin wrote many ragtime songs. Listen now as Joshua Rifkin plays Joplin's "Maple Leaf Rag."

(MUSIC)

VOICE ONE:

African-American and Creole musicians in New Orleans, Louisiana probably developed the first true jazz music. This happened during the early nineteen-hundreds. Musicians performing in memorial and holiday parades added their own music to written music. This New Orleans music is often called classic, traditional or Dixieland jazz.

From New Orleans, musicians such as Jelly Roll Morton, Sidney Bechet and King Oliver helped spread jazz to other places. King Oliver's Creole Jazz Band plays "Chimes Blues."

(MUSIC)

III. Listen and choose the best answer to each question you hear.

1. How was the history of jazz presented to the public in 2001?
2. What kind of music does jazz mean?
3. How does a jazz musician surprise listeners?
4. Who is the writer of "Maple Leaf Rag"?
5. Which band plays "Chimes Blues" on the recording?

Text Two

VOICE ONE:

Jazz continued to gain popularity as the years passed. During the nineteen-twenties, Louis Armstrong became famous for his performances on the trumpet and jazz cornet. Later his unusual voice became just as famous. Listen as Louis Armstrong and his Hot Five play "West End Blues."

(MUSIC)

VOICE TWO:

Historians often call the nineteen-twenties the Jazz Age, or the Golden Age of American Jazz. Young people from the Middle West created a new musical form during this time. People called this Chicago-style jazz. These musicians included great performers like Gene Krupa and Benny Goodman.

During this Golden Age, Bix Beiderbecke played cornet solos with the Paul Whiteman Orchestra. He also played piano and wrote music. Here he plays "There Ain't No Sweet Man (Worth the Salt of My Tears)" with the Paul Whiteman Orchestra.

(MUSIC)

VOICE ONE:

As time passed, a jazz form called "swing" became very popular in America. People danced to swing music until after World War Two. This musical form got its name from a song by Duke Ellington. Listen as Duke Ellington and his orchestra play "Sing, Sing, Sing (with a Swing). "

(MUSIC)

VOICE TWO:

Benny Goodman led one of America's most successful swing bands. People called Goodman "The King of Swing." Critics also praised his playing of the clarinet. He was the first jazz clarinetist to play with symphony orchestras. Goodman also presented black and white jazz musicians playing together for the first time. He introduced great African-American jazz artists like Lionel Hampton and Teddy Wilson.

Other big bands of the time were led by Jimmy Dorsey and Tommy Dorsey, Earl Hines, Artie Shaw, Stan Kenton and Glenn Miller. Fine jazz singers performed with these bands. They included Nat "King" Cole, Ella Fitzgerald, Sarah Vaughn and Billie Holiday. Listen now as Billie Holiday sings "Solitude."

(MUSIC)

VOICE ONE:

After World War Two, a new kind of music replaced swing as the most popular jazz. Next week, we will tell you about this kind called bebop. Until then, we leave you with the Glenn Miller Orchestra playing "String of Pearls."

(MUSIC)

VOICE TWO:

This program was written by Jerilyn Watson. It was produced by Cynthia Kirk. Our studio engineer was Holly Capehart. I'm Shirley Griffith.

VOICE ONE:

And I'm Steve Ember. Join us again next week for the second part of our report about the history of jazz on the VOA Special English program, This Is America.

(MUSIC)

Part Four Here's More

Exercise One

The Olympics are held every four years in a different city in the world. Athletes from many countries compete in a variety of sports which are divided into winter and summer games.

The Olympics began in Greece more than 2,700 years ago. The games were originally part of a religious festival in honor of the Greek Gods. Eventually, the games became the most important festival in all of Greece.

The first recorded Olympic competition was held in 776 B.C. It was held in an outdoor stadium which was about 200 meters long and 30 meters wide. The stadium was in a valley, and about 40,000 people watched the event. The first 13 Olympics consisted of only one race — running.

Since 776 B.C. the games had been held regularly for about 1,200 years. In the year 397 the Olympics were prohibited by the Roman Emperor.

It was not until 1896 that the first Olympics of modern times were held in Athens. From then on the games are held every four years regularly. The Olympics have become the world's most important athletic events and a symbol of the sporting friendship of all the people of the world.

Exercise Two

1. Why start with classical? Well, many people think that music was pretty much perfected several centuries ago and everything since is crap. Classical music is complex and layered and beautiful but it is not spontaneous. Spontaneity is very important in music I think.
2. It is the newest form of music out there. People often call jazz the only American Art form ... I would tend to agree with this but hip hop is a close second place. Beats, Rhymes, Life ... what else could you want?
3. Bands that play the blues are usually not very good. The blues is a personal thing, and should usually be played by some guy who is very ugly and is half full of whiskey. Without this how can you have the blues ... can good-looking people get the blues?
4. It is very hard to argue with rock & roll. In many ways it is a lot like Christianity. It involves icon with long hair, and people have been predicting and attempting to initiate its demise since it began.
5. This type of music is for people who don't know anything about music. This is perfectly all right though, because dance music is for dancing, not for contemplating.
6. Some people call it the music of the people. Something that everyone can relate to some sort of common experience. If you have something to say and you want to put music to your thoughts, that is folk.

Unit 6 Thanksgiving Holiday

Part Two Listen Now

Text One

(MUSIC)

VOICE ONE:

Welcome to This Is America in VOA Special English. I'm Faith Lapidus.

VOICE TWO:

And I'm Steve Ember. The story of the Thanksgiving holiday is our report this week.

VOICE ONE:

This Thursday is Thanksgiving Day. Thanksgiving is celebrated every year on the fourth Thursday of November. The month of November is in autumn, the main season for harvesting crops.

The writer O. Henry called Thanksgiving the one holiday that is purely American. It is not a religious holiday. But it has spiritual meaning.

Some Americans travel long distances to be with their families. They eat a large dinner, which is the main part of the celebration. For many people, Thanksgiving is the only time when all members of a family gather. The holiday is a time of family reunion.

VOICE TWO:

Alma Scott-Buczak gathers her family for Thanksgiving dinner every year. She welcomes about thirty people to her home in northern New Jersey, near New York City.

Guests sit at several tables. Children eat together at their own table. Many people who are invited are relatives. But anyone can bring a friend.

Ms. Scott-Buczak serves the traditional American Thanksgiving dinner. But she adds a few special foods that are especially popular in some African-American homes, dishes like sweet potato pie and corn pudding.

Before the meal begins, the people all say a few words about what they are most thankful for.

VOICE ONE:

The family of Ismaila Sanghua of Silver Spring, Maryland, also eats a large Thanksgiving dinner. It comes just weeks after their big dinner that celebrated the Muslim holiday of Eid al-Fitr, the end of the observance of Ramadan.

Mr. Sanghua was born in Sierra Leone. He says the family began a Thanksgiving tradition because the children, ages nine through sixteen, wanted to celebrate an American holiday.

VOA producer, writer and editor Subhash Vohra was born in India. Mr. Vohra has been a journalist there and in Britain and Germany. He says he is pleased to take part in the traditions of places where he lives. He says he, his wife and two daughters have been enjoying an American Thanksgiving holiday meal in this country for many years.

VOICE TWO:

Listen now as the Paul Hillier Singers present an early-American song of thanks, "Give Good Gifts One to Another."

(MUSIC)

Text Two

VOICE ONE:

Joan and Sandy Horwitt of Arlington, Virginia, have been holding a Thanksgiving dinner for almost thirty years. All the guests bring food to share. The Horwitts started this tradition when they moved to Virginia from the Midwest.

They regretted not being able to be with all their family members. But they soon met new friends. So they started a holiday dinner for others who were also unable to travel to family homes for the holiday.

At first, many people brought their babies and young children. Now some of the first guests are grandparents.

Mr. and Mrs. Horwitt serve a turkey as the center of the meal. So do many other Americans. Most people serve it with a cooked bread mixture inside.

VOICE TWO:

This year, some Americans asked poultry companies if it's all right to eat turkey. These people feared bird flu, a disease that has struck birds in Asia and Europe. But public officials say no turkeys in the United States have been infected with the deadly kind of avian influenza.

Other traditional Thanksgiving foods served with turkey are potatoes, a cooked fruit called cranberries and pumpkin pie. Many people eat more at Thanksgiving than at any other time of the year.

Some families serve other meats besides turkey. And some American homes have vegetarian Thanksgiving dinners. This means no meat is served.

VOICE ONE:

Over the years, Americans have added new traditions to their Thanksgiving celebration. For example, a number of professional and college football games are played on Thanksgiving Day. Some of the games are broadcast on national television.

Many people also like to watch Thanksgiving Day parades on television. Big stores in several cities organize these parades. For example, Macy's has a very famous Thanksgiving Day parade in New York.

III. Listen and choose the best answer to each question you hear.

1. How long have the Horwitts been holding a Thanksgiving dinner?
2. For whom did the Horwitts start the holiday dinner?
3. What is a turkey usually served with?
4. When cooking Thanksgiving dinner, what were Americans afraid of this year?
5. Whose name is "Macy's"?

Part Four Here's More

Exercise

1. In Massachusetts, Governor Mitt Romney has proposed to buy a low-cost computer for every middle and high school student in his state.
2. More women are becoming national leaders. The newest include Angela Merkel. She is expected to become the first female chancellor of Germany on Tuesday.
3. The group found that one in five children suffered from malnutrition in the Zinder area in August.
4. Our listener question this week comes from Vietnam. Thai Thu Thu asks about the Grand Canyon in the southwestern state of Arizona.
5. The ships are carrying food, medicine and other supplies. It will take them at least two days to reach islands of Tikipia, Anuta and Fataka.
6. Only one painting sold at this show. It was a famous work called "Lavender Mist." This painting now hangs in the National Gallery of Art in Washington, DC.
7. Local radio stations like Washington, DC's WKYS have been helping the singer host the contests in each city, but the details surrounding his visits are kept secret.
8. English football club Liverpool crashed out of the Champions League on Tuesday, despite fighting back from a 3-0 deficit to tie FC Basel 3-3 in Switzerland.

9. Building after building under water. Refugees in shelters. Thousands of others unsure where to go. This is what one of America's historic cities was reduced to this week by a powerful storm, Katrina.
10. When no major record company would offer Jay Z a contract, he co-founded Roca-a-Fella Records just to get his music heard.
11. In *Red Meat Cures Cancer*, Starbuck O'Dwyer tells the story of Sky Thorne, a top executive at what you might call the worst of all possible fast food chains, a company called Tailburger.
12. Ruth Brown is often thought to be the first Rhythm and Blues singer. She was extremely popular in the nineteen fifties. And she is still singing today! We leave you now with her singing "Lucky Lips."
13. Visitors at the festival also saw a play called "Sonia Flew" by Melinda Lopez. An American family is celebrating Christmas and Hanukkah in two thousand one.

Unit 7

Studying Abroad

Part Two Listen Now

Text One

I'm Faith Lapidus with the VOA Special English Education Report.

We talked last week about the number of Americans studying in foreign countries. This week, our subject is foreign students in the United States. More than five hundred sixty-five thousand attended American colleges and universities during the last school year.

The Institute of International Education, based in New York, recently published its yearly report, "Open Doors Two Thousand Five." The report says the number of foreign students decreased by about one percent during the school year that began last fall. That was less of a decrease than the year before, when the number fell by almost two and a half percent.

India sent the most students, more than eighty thousand. That was a one percent increase from the year before. China sent the next highest number, more than sixty-two thousand. That was also a one percent increase. South Korea was third, with more than fifty-three thousand students, up two percent. Japan was fourth, with more than forty-two thousand students, an increase of three percent.

The report says one hundred forty-five American colleges and universities had one thousand or more international students last year. The school with the largest number was the University of Southern California, in Los Angeles. It had almost seven thousand international students. The University of Illinois at Urbana-Champaign was second with more than five thousand five hundred.

The recent decrease in the number of international students is seen as a result of several things. These include difficulties getting a student visa, especially in scientific and technical areas. They also include higher costs as well as competition from schools in other English-speaking countries and in students' home countries.

Assistant Secretary of State Dina Habib Powell says international students are welcome in the

United States. In her words, "The United States remains the best place in the world" to seek higher education.

You can read more of the report on the Web site of the Institute of International Education: iie.org. And you can get information about how to study in the United States from our Foreign Student Series. Go to voaspecialenglish.com. Enter the words "foreign student" with quotation marks in the search box, then click on Archive.

This VOA Special English Education Report was written by Nancy Steinbach.

III. Listen and choose the best answer to each question you hear.

1. How many foreign students attended American colleges and universities during the last school year?
2. Which country has sent the largest number of students to America?
3. Which of the following is NOT a reason for the recent decrease in the number of international students?

Text Two

I'm Gwen Outen with the VOA Special English Education Report.

We continue our reports for students around the world who want to attend a college or university in the United States. This week, we answer questions from two listeners. Richard Lin from China wants to know how to get a scholarship to an American college. Amarkhuu Ayulguisaikhan of Mongolia wants to know the differences among different kinds of financial aid. They are assistantships, grants, scholarships and fellowships.

An assistantship is a job a student does. In exchange, the student receives money or attends classes for free. Graduate students usually get assistantships. The student works about twenty hours a week helping a professor. The student may teach classes, help grade papers and tests, or do research in a laboratory.

A grant is a gift of money to pay for some or all of the costs of college. Unlike loans, grants do not have to be re-paid. Private groups or organizations generally give grants to students who need the money.

Scholarships and fellowships also do not have to be re-paid. A scholarship is financial aid to undergraduate students; a fellowship is the same kind of aid for graduate students. Generally, scholarships and fellowships go to students with special abilities or athletic skills. Some scholarships are based on financial need. Others go to students who live in a certain area.

For example, the University of Missouri in Columbia has two financial aid programs for international students only. The Global Tiger Scholarship is supported by the group representing former university students. In return for scholarship money, the international student agrees to help the group during the school year. The other international scholarship or fellowship at the University of Missouri is called the Grant-in-Aid Program. It provides money to students who need the help, get good grades and take part in university activities.

To get these scholarships, students must complete forms found on the university's Web site. The address is missouri.edu. Information about scholarships from other colleges and universities is listed on their own Web sites.

For general information about how to get financial aid, go to a Web site called FinAid. The address is finaid.org.

This VOA Special English Education Report was written by Nancy Steinbach. This is Gwen Outen.

Part Four Here's More

Exercise

The United States has a large, varied, and innovative system of higher education.

It is large. America has more than 2,300 four-year, degree-granting colleges and universities. There are also more than 1,800 two-year institutions and community colleges.

It is varied. The schools of the Ivy League are certainly well-known, and many Chinese students aspire to attend these seven world-class private universities. Also private are such great universities as Stanford University, the University of Chicago, New York University, and the University of Southern California. Private universities originally founded by religious congregations are another large sector. Among the most noted would be Georgetown University, Baylor University, Brigham Young University, and the University of Notre Dame. And besides these "name" schools there are many others.

Fewer Chinese students initially concentrate on the tremendous educational power of the 50 state university systems which educate about 80 percent of American students. Each state, depending on its size, has an array of schools — comprehensive universities, universities that emphasize science and engineering, liberal arts colleges, and community colleges. Some states have military colleges and maritime universities. The old teacher's colleges and agricultural schools have become comprehensive universities. So too have most of the old "branch campuses."

America's system of higher education is innovative in two aspects. The first is that American higher education is moving through a creative period of innovation. There is a new emphasis on flexible curricula and flexible scheduling. Distance learning and continuing education — especially education for professionals in health care, law enforcement, and business, for instance — are flourishing. MBA programs that meet on weekends or during the summer have become popular.

The second is that in every field at every level it emphasizes creativity, critical thinking skills, and the ability to challenge authority and prevailing paradigms.

The returned Chinese students all agree that their greatest challenge was the transition to a classroom where students ask questions, reply to questions, and state and defend points of view. Students challenge and defend one another's papers in graduate seminars. Later, their research and papers must go through peer review. The returned students are all unanimous in saying that — after the initial classroom shock — learning these creative thinking and presentation skills was the greatest reward of their time of study in the United States. At a time when China has embraced opening and reform, there can be no greater need.

Unit 8 Bird Flu

Part Two Listen Now

Text One

The World Health Organization says it is worried people may stop eating chicken because of the growing concern about bird flu. During the mad cow scare, sales of beef plummeted. WHO spokesman Ian Simpson tells VOA there is no need to panic.

"At this stage, there is no evidence of anyone having become sick, anyone becoming infected with avian influenza as a result of eating properly cooked, properly prepared meat and egg from poultry," said Mr. Simpson. "So, there is no reason to stop eating chicken. There is no reason to stop eating eggs. But, there is every reason to insure that any chicken meat, any poultry meat or any eggs that are consumed are properly prepared and properly cooked."

The World Health Organization says thorough cooking will kill any virus, including the deadly H5N1 strain of avian flu. Eggs from sick birds could also contain the virus. So, the World Health Organization advises people from affected areas not to eat raw, or undercooked eggs.

The UN health agency says birds from diseased flocks should not enter the food chain, and infected birds should not be used for animal feed. But, the World Health Organization says consumers run no risk of getting the virus through handling or eating poultry in areas where there is no bird flu outbreak.

Mr. Simpson says people in affected areas often are exposed to the H5N1 virus during the slaughtering and subsequent handling of diseased or dead birds. He says people can take precautionary measures.

"For example, if people are preparing them, they should ideally be wearing protection of their face, and also protection of their hands," he added. "That the area where they are preparing them should be a hygienic area. It should be able to be completely cleaned, so that, at the end of the day, or at the end of the shift, when the chickens have been prepared, that all of the waste material is gotten rid of safely and hygienically, so that the waste material does not pose any risk to people coming into the area afterwards."

The World Health Organization says raw meat should be separated from cooked or ready-to-eat foods to avoid contamination. It says people preparing food in areas with avian flu outbreaks should wash hands frequently, and all surfaces and utensils that have been in contact with raw meat should be washed and disinfected.

Text Two

The EU says it has extended a ban on the importation of birds and feathers from most of Russia. EU spokesperson Pia Ahrenkilde Hansen spoke of Russian and EU efforts.

"The Russian veterinary services have implemented all necessary measures to avoid the spread of the disease," she said. "As far as the standing committee on the food chain and animal health meeting today is concerned, that committee this morning has endorsed the ban on pet birds and feathers from Siberia to cover the whole territory with the exception of Kaliningrad, Karelia, Murmansk and St. Petersburg."

The EU decision followed the discovery of the bird flu virus in the Russian village of Yandovka, several hundred kilometers south of Moscow. Residents reported sudden deaths among their domesticated fowl, prompting Russian authorities to impose a quarantine around the village and to destroy all chickens, ducks and geese in the area. This is the first time that the bird flu virus has been detected in western Russia, prompting fears that the pathogen, believed to be carried from region to region by migratory birds, could spread to other parts of Europe.

Ms. Ahrenkilde Hansen said a preliminary test on a sample from a Greek island came back negative, but more tests were needed.

Elsewhere, officials in Thailand say, a 48-year-old farmer in the western part of the country has died after handling and eating diseased fowl. The man became Thailand's 13th confirmed human death from bird flu, which so far has shown a limited capacity to jump from birds to humans, but has yet to spread by human-to-human contact. At least 120 people have contracted the bird flu virus in southeast Asia in the past two years, resulting in at least 60 deaths in Thailand, Vietnam, Cambodia and Indonesia.

In China, Foreign Ministry Spokesman Kong Quan said the spread of the bird flu within his nation appears to have been contained, after more than 90,000 birds were culled from a farm in Inner Mongolia, where thousands of chickens and ducks succumbed to the virus.

"After receiving a report of suspected bird flu in Inner Mongolia, the Chinese Agriculture Ministry immediately sent a working team to guide the local prevention and control work," he said. "Local governments and sanitary organizations have also taken emergency measures to quarantine, seal or kill and disinfect in accordance to the regulations. Now the epidemic situation is under control and no new infection areas have been found."

The number of nations and regions dealing with the virus has continued to grow, with nations in Africa, the Middle East and elsewhere bracing for possible outbreaks among bird populations in the future.

Part Four Here's More

Exercise

Every people has its own special words and expressions. And one of the most interesting kinds of words in the English language is the acronym. An acronym is a word that is formed from the first letters of several other words. For example, OPEC is an acronym for the Organization of Petroleum Exporting Countries. And an initialism is like an acronym, but it does not sound like a real word itself. Instead, it just states the first letters of other words. USA is an initialism for the United States of America. UN is an initialism for the United Nations.

Acronym and initialism are like language brothers, and both can be an easy way to shorten the title or name that has many words. It is easier to say VOA than the Voice of America. But the same acronym or initialism may represent different organizations, groups or names. For example, the Voice of America is not the only organization with the initialism VOA. The Volkswagen of America Automobile Company uses the same three letters. So does the Volunteers of America Organization that helps poor people. This has been a growing problem for English speakers. Political leaders, scientists and others have invented thousands of acronyms to describe everything from tax legislation to space vehicles. The great American writer H. L. Mencken observed correctly that many Americans feel a strong desire to reduce complete names or ideas to the shortest possible form. Most of the world thinks that the acronym NATO only means the North Atlantic Treaty Organization. However, the same acronym also can mean the National Association of Theaters Owners in the United States. You cannot be sure that the member of the PLO belongs to the Palestine Liberation Organization. He may really be a member of the Philippine Labor Organization or he may be a scientist, helping to launch a rocket in the Pacific Ocean as part of the Pacific Launch Operation of the American Space Program.

Do not feel bad if you find it difficult to follow so many acronyms and initialisms. You are not alone.

Back in 1960, a group of language experts made a list of all the acronyms they could find in the English Language. Their list contained about 12,000. These days, however, the number of the acronyms on the list has increased more than ten times. There are more than 100,000 different acronyms.

So, it is clear that acronyms and initialisms have become a permanent part of the English language. And the one I like best is MJ. Those letters do not represent Marine Jet, Master of Journalism or Military Judge. They are just me, Mas Joyce.

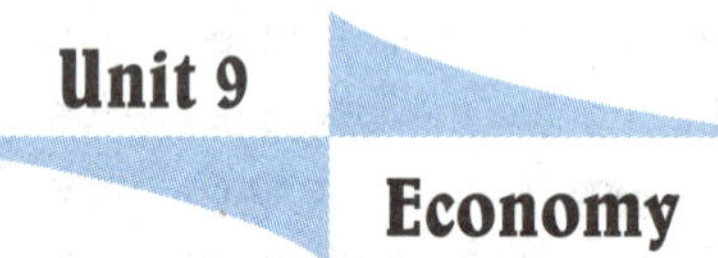

Unit 9 Economy

Part Two Listen Now

Text One

The Indians say the Japanese have failed to take advantage of India's soaring economy.

At a time when India's economy is growing by nearly 10 percent a year, Japan's share of total Indian trade fell below 2.6 percent in the 2005–2006 fiscal year, compared with nearly four percent several years earlier.

Japanese officials say their country ranks as the third largest foreign investor in India. But Indian businessmen say the Japanese have not followed up with sufficient new investment.

At the India-Japan Strategic Partnership Symposium in New Delhi on Friday, Rakesh Mohan, deputy governor of the Reserve Bank of India, reminded Japanese business leaders they were responsible for helping to build a world-class automotive industry here.

He says those manufacturing standards have spread to other sectors of India's economy, but further investment from Japan has been disappointing.

"The whole total quality movement in India has been induced by Japan and therefore, I think, that there have been a lot of opportunities missed," said Mohan. "And one would hope that now Japan would no longer miss such opportunities in the years to come."

Mikio Sasaki, the chairman of Mitsubishi Corporation, Japan's largest trading company, told the symposium that India has much to do if it desires significant new foreign investment.

"Developing power-generating plants, ports, roads, railways and other public infrastructure is a major area that needs a strong response," he said.

Japanese investors also complain about bureaucratic delays, widespread corruption, and interstate regulations that increase the time and cost of moving goods across the country.

Indian business leaders counter that they face significant challenges in expanding exports to Japan, such as entry barriers for chemicals and medicines, and high tariffs on seafood.

The two countries are in the process of reaching what they call a "comprehensive economic partnership agreement." The Japanese say the first high-level dialogue on the pact will be held in Japan next month. An Indian official predicts a deal will be made within one year.

Text Two

Leaders from Asia and Africa stressed the need for both continents to fully partake of the benefits of globalization by pushing for closer economic ties and trade between the two continents.

More than 40 heads of state from both continents have traveled to Jakarta to participate in the Asian-African Summit that begins Friday.

Indonesian President Susilo Bambang Yudhoyono told heads of state at a business conference being held a day before the summit the countries of both continents need to band together for economic strength.

"In the days to come with the new Asia-Africa strategic partnership in operation, the countries of both continents can work more effectively together to help build a more equitable world financial and economic architecture. We can also have a bigger voice in the reforms of multi-lateral institutes, including the United Nations, the World Bank, and the World Trade Organization."

Foreign Ministers of more than 80 Asian and African countries approved a draft that their leaders will discuss during the two-day summit aimed at renewing the partnership between the two continents that began 50 years ago.

That first summit was held in 1955 in the Indonesian city of Bandung where African and Asian leaders met to put their colonial past behind them and take their place on the world stage.

Although five decades have passed, Nigerian President Olusegun Obasanjo says little has changed for Africa and the globalization of the West has lent little benefit to his continent.

"The new globalization has little or no regard for culture, history, values, and the dreams of the weak. Its god is money and profit at the expense of almost all else. There is hardly an attempt to relate products and institutions to local specificities, hence it generates resistance and rejection, rather than acceptance."

Mr. Obasanjo stressed the need for cooperation between Africa and Asia in order for the two continents to reap the benefits of globalization.

"Partnership between Asian and African private sector operatives should be an obvious alternative to total dependence on the developed countries. The low level of business relationship between business interests in both continents must be addressed considering the wide range of opportunities that exist and the common values and experiences that we all share."

China weighed in with President Hu Jintao pointing out the great economic strides his country has made.

Mr. Hu said China was eager to share its experience of economic development to help other countries and looked forward to developing stronger economic ties with Africa.

IV. Listen and choose the best answer to each question you hear.

1. Which of the following is NOT a current reason for the cooperation between Asian and African countries?
2. Where was the first Asian-African Summit held in 1955?
3. Why has the economic globalization had little benefit to Asian and African countries according to their leaders?

Part Four Here's More

Exercise

1. The United States Defense Secretary Donald Rumsfeld has arrived in Britain for talks with the British Prime Minister Tony Blair on situation in Iraq and Afghanistan.
2. The American Secretary of State Colin Powell is holding talks in Damascus today with the Syrian President Bashar al-Asad.
3. President Bush has given a task of creating an interregnum Iraqi government to a former diplomat Paul Bremer.
4. The American singer Michael Jackson is suing the Motown record label for money he says he has owned in royalties for several classic songs.
5. Secretary General of NATO George Robinson held talks with Russian President Putin and senior government ministers.
6. The European Union's foreign policy chief Javie Solana has had meetings on the new Middle East peace initiative with the Palestinian leader Yasser Arafat and the Palestinian Prime Minister.
7. The Israeli Prime Minister Ariel Sharon has met his Palestinian counterpart Mahmoud Abbas, also known as Abu Mazen, in Jerusalem for the first time to discuss the American-backed peace plan, known as the Road Map.
8. A veteran American journalist Andrew Mildred has been deported from Zimbabwe after being categorized by the government as a prohibited immigrant.
9. The Algerian Prime Minister Ahmed Ouyahia has said the number of people killed in an earthquake in the north of the country has risen to at least 450.
10. The United Nations Secretary General Kofi Annan has named Sergio Vieira de Mello as the special representative for Iraq for an initial four months period.

Unit 10 Massage

Part Two Listen Now

Text One

Massage therapists are on hand nearly every day at the M. D. Anderson Cancer Center, which is part of the University of Texas Medical Center here in Houston. They provide a therapy that is aimed not so much at curing the disease, but at alleviating the stress and emotional fatigue of their patients.

Cancer patient Celeste was a believer in the benefits of massage before being diagnosed and is an even bigger believer now.

Celeste: There is something about another person touching you that ... it just makes you feel good. And that it can give you hope, you know that they are not scared of you, you know just because you have cancer.

Celeste says many people are afraid of cancer and those who have it. She says her own family members even had trouble saying the word for a long time after she told them that she had a malignant tumor in her throat. She says her longtime massage therapist turned her away.

Celeste: When I got diagnosed, I called my regular massage therapist that I was going to and she refused to massage me because I had cancer. And I told her that my doctor said it was okay, but she said "no, I was taught that." You don't want to massage anyone with cancer because it could spread the cancer.

Medical experts say there is no risk to cancer patients from massage, as long as the therapist avoids the area of the body where the cancer is present. M. D. Anderson Cancer Center is working with massage therapists in the Houston area to educate them about cancer and to let them know they can provide services to cancer patients.

Massage therapist Curtis Beinhorn, who works full-time at M. D. Anderson, says cancer patients need massage more than those who are healthy.

Curtis Beinhorn: Many patients feel fatigue, nausea, pain and anxiety. They have psycho-social issues that surround them as well as their families and massage takes a lot of that stress away. It helps them to relax.

III. Listen and choose the best answer to each question you hear.

1. Which statement is NOT true about the M. D. Anderson Cancer Center?
2. What happened to Celeste after she got cancer?
3. In what condition can cancer patients have a safe massage?

Text Two

M. D. Anderson, which is recognized around the world for its advanced cancer treatments, introduced massage and other non-standard therapies partly because research had shown their effectiveness. But M. D. Anderson Wellness Center administrator Laura Baynham-Fletcher says it was also in response to patient demand.

Laura Baynham-Fletcher: We did a survey of our patients and about 80 percent of the patients here at Anderson who responded to the survey stated that they were engaging in some type of complementary therapy, whether it be a spiritual practice they brought to cancer or something that they started doing as a result of their diagnosis.

Other complementary therapies now being offered at M. D. Anderson include acupuncture, special diet and exercise programs and herbal medicines. But Laura Baynham-Fletcher says these therapies should not be seen as alternatives to conventional therapies.

Laura Baynham-Fletcher: We actually look at these therapies as complementary, so we don't even use the term *alternative* because that implies that these therapies might be used instead of conventional therapies.

Conventional cancer treatments include chemotherapy and radiation, both of which can produce debilitating side effects. Curtis Beinhorn says patients provide constant testimony to the efficacy of massage in reducing these maladies.

Curtis Beinhorn: We always take note of what they say, and it's ... it's very nice to hear that ... they always leave notes about how wonderful they felt, how they were able to relax, how they were able to get some sleep the night afterwards, that it made such a big difference to be able to feel connected again.

Massage therapy is now recognized by the American Cancer Society as an important complementary therapy for cancer patients. M. D. Anderson Cancer Center is also working with a university in Shanghai, China to study and test other ancient therapies that may also help people who are fighting a disease like cancer.

Greg Flakus, VOA news.

Part Four Here's More

Exercise One

1. American government scientists say they have successfully tested a vaccine that protects people against avian influenza, or bird flu.
2. There is no cure for Parkinson's disease. Mostly it is treated with drugs to increase the amount of dopamine in the brain.
3. Most lung cancer deaths are caused by tobacco use. But smokers are not the only ones at risk. So are people who breathe tobacco smoke in the air.
4. The first cases of SARS were discovered in Guangdong province, in southern China in November of two thousand two. It is believed to have crossed from animals to people. Many questions remain about how the virus first appeared and when it might appear again.

Exercise Two

1. Flu is an infectious illness which is like a very bad cold, but which causes a fever.
2. Obesity is the condition of being too fat in a way that is dangerous to health.
3. Insomnia is the condition of not being able to sleep over a period of time.
4. Diabetes is a disease in which the body cannot control the level of sugar in the blood.
5. AIDS is a serious disease caused by a virus which destroys the body's natural protection from infection, and which usually causes death.
6. Heart attack is a serious medical condition in which the heart does not get enough blood, causing great pain and often leading to death.
7. TB or tuberculosis is a serious disease which is infectious and can attack many parts of a person's body, especially their lungs.

Unit 11 Sports Events

Part Two Listen Now

Text One

A crowd of some 35,000, including US First Lady Laura Bush and Italian film legend Sophia Loren, filled the Olympic Stadium. More than 4,700 performers, including fast-moving skaters with fiery rocket packs, dancers and even dancing cows opened the festivities.

Some 2,600 athletes from more than 80 countries and territories marched into the stadium accompanied by American pop music from the 1970s and 1980s. The worldwide television audience was estimated at around two billion.

Following more than two hours of celebration and pageantry, International Olympic Committee President Jacques Rogge addressed the athletes.

"Please compete in the spirit of fair play, mutual understanding, and respect," he said. "And above all, please compete cleanly by refusing doping."

Then, the President of the Italian Republic, Carlo Azeglio Ciampi officially opened the Games.

"I declare open in Turin the celebration of the 20th Winter Olympic Games," he said.

The musical highlights of the show included an appearance by the late John Lennon's wife, Yoko Ono, and his song "Imagine" sung by Peter Gabriel.

The entertainment was capped off with a performance by legendary Italian tenor Luciano Pavarotti.

The final torch bearer was former cross country skier Stefania Belmondo of Italy. She lit the tallest-ever Olympic cauldron, which rises to 57 meters. It will be seen throughout the city during the 16 days of competition, as athletes vie for 84 gold medals in 15 sports.

The Olympics are being protected by unprecedented security, which includes some 15,000 Italian police and a no-fly zone backed up by NATO fighter jets.

III. Listen and choose the best answer to each question you hear.

1. Which of the following people was NOT present at the opening ceremony of 2006 Winter Olympics?
2. How many performers opened the festivities?
3. What was the most attractive performance during the opening celebration at the 20th Winter Olympics?
4. Which of the following statements about the Olympic torch is NOT true?

Text Two

Germany had never lost in 14 previous matches played here in Dortmund over 71 years, and Italy had never lost a match to Germany in a World Cup, with two wins and two draws, so something had to give.

Both teams played with intensity, going end to end for 90 minutes and nearly all of the 30 minutes of extra time without finding the net.

Germany had won its quarterfinal against Argentina on penalty kicks, and just when it seemed this scoreless battle would be headed for a shootout, Italy struck twice in the closing moments of extra time.

Defender Fabio Grosso blasted in a shot from the right side of the box into the upper left corner of the goal, and barely more than a minute later, just before the final whistle, forward Alessandro del Piero broke free on a counterattack and scored to put an exclamation point on the victory.

Italian coach Marcelo Lippi, through an interpreter, said he believed his team deserved the victory. "In my opinion we controlled the match. We didn't get so many chances, but the match didn't give so many chances. But in other way, we controlled the match, and I'm really, really happy with all the effort of my players, because, after all we played also against 50,000 people, the German supporters who were fantastic and we scored two excellent goals, which avoided us to come to the penalty kicks, and you know that this is always a lottery."

Klinsmann was proud of his German team, a team which had not been expected to even reach the quarterfinals at this World Cup. "We can only make compliments to that team. It's a very young team. They did great. They did fantastic throughout the whole tournament. Also before the tournament, the preparation. I mean it's amazing the spirit that they show, the character, and they gave all their heart and all their passion and everything there was in them, and I think they made our whole country really proud."

The Germans are not done at the tournament. They will play for third place on Saturday against the loser of Wednesday night's semifinal between France and Portugal. The winner of that match will meet Italy for the World Cup title on Sunday in Berlin.

Part Four Here's More

Exercise

No other sporting event captures the world's imagination like the FIFA World Cup. Ever since the first tentative competition in Uruguay in 1930, FIFA has constantly grown in popularity and prestige.

A group of French football administrators, led in the 1920s by the innovative Jules Rimet, are credited with the original idea of bringing the world's strongest national football teams together to compete for the title of World Champions. But the Second World War put a 12-year stop to the competition.

When it resumed, the FIFA World Cup rapidly advanced to its undisputed status as the greatest single sporting event of the modern world. Held since 1958 alternately in Europe and the Americas, the World Cup broke new ground with the Executive Committee's decision in May 1996 to select Korea and Japan as co-hosts for the 2002 edition.

Since 1930, the 16 tournaments have seen only seven different winners. However, the FIFA World Cup has also been punctuated by dramatic upsets that have helped create football history — the United States defeating England in 1950, North Korea's defeat of Italy in 1966 , Cameroon's emergence in the 1980s and their opening match defeat of the Argentinean cup-holders in 1990 ...

Today, the FIFA World Cup holds the entire global public under its spell. An accumulated audience of over 3.7 billion people watched the France 98 tournament, including approximately 1.3 billion for the final alone, while over 2.7 million people flocked to watch the 64 matches in the French stadium.

After all these years and so many changes, however, the main focus of the FIFA World Cup remains the same — the glistening golden trophy, which is the embodiment of every footballer's ambition.

Unit 12 Around the World

Part Two Listen Now

Text One

First stop, Iraq — where insurgents carried out new attacks Tuesday. Baghdad governor Ali al-Haidri and one of his bodyguards were killed in a road ambush. And in Baghdad's green zone, a truck bomb killed 10 people. Iraqi officials say continued terrorism will not deter the country from holding elections on January 30th.

"We'd like to ensure that we continue on the path to freedom and bring stability back to Iraq. They will try to stop this process but we will not allow them to."

Also in the Middle East. A violent exchange in Northern Gaza. Seven Palestinians were killed by Israeli tank fire Tuesday, according to Palestinian sources. Israel said the tank fired in response to a Palestinian mortar attack on an Israeli target. The exchange came just days before the upcoming Palestinian elections to replace the late Yasser Arafat — a step some are hoping may revive peace talks.

In Canada, officials announced a new case of mad cow disease, the country's second case in more than a decade. The Canadian Food Inspection Agency said Sunday that a cow from Alberta tested positive for bovine spongiform encephalopathy — the scientific name for the brain-wasting disease that can infect people who eat meat from infected animals. But if you're a meat eater, Canadian officials say not to worry. No part of the animal entered the human food or animal feed systems. From a public health perspective, this finding does not threaten the safety of Canadian beef.

III. Listen and choose the best answer to each question you hear.

1. How many people were reported killed in Baghdad?
2. On which day were seven Palestinians reported killed by Israeli tank fire?
3. Why did the Canadian officials say that meat eaters needn't worry about mad cow disease?

Text Two

Severe flooding in several countries tops our international headlines. Northwestern England is recovering from the worst flooding it's seen in 40 years. Flood warnings remain in effect throughout the UK. A similar scene in Brazil, where torrential rains have lashed São Paulo causing deadly landslides. And a national emergency has been declared in Costa Rica, where heavy rainfall has displaced thousands of people along the Atlantic coast.

Firefighters in South Australia continue to battle the most deadly wildfire to ravage the country in more than 20 years. At least nine people have been killed by the fire, which has burned through hundreds of thousands of acres since Monday.

It was just like a fire storm of whirling winds of flames that just came through, and things just started bursting into flames around.

Fueled by strong winds and temperatures in excess of 111 degrees Fahrenheit, the fire has forced many residents to flee their homes.

In Canada, officials have announced the second case of mad cow disease in less than a month. They say the discovery was made during a stepped-up testing program, and the case poses no danger to consumers.

The carcass is under CFIA control and once again no part of this animal entered either the human or animal food chain.

Part Four Here's More

Exercise One

A report in a Spanish newspaper says Spanish authorities had uncovered plans for a terrorist attack on New York's Grand Central Station.

"El Mundo" says that while investigating last year's Madrid train bombings, investigators found a sketch and computer data of Grand Central at a suspect's home. US and Spanish officials are downplaying the report, saying it's not even clear whether the sketch depicts Grand Central.

Exercise Two

In Iraq, officials are investigating the fatal shooting of a judge and his son Tuesday in Baghdad. The two were working for the tribunal that will put Saddam Hussein and members of his former government on trial. They were gunned down a day after the tribunal announced that one of Saddam's half-brothers would be the first to face trial on human rights charges.

Exercise Three

A teenage Muslim girl has won the right to wear full Islamic dress at her British school. An appeal court ruled Wednesday that her religious rights were violated when the school refused to let her wear a jilbab — which covers the whole body except for the hands and face.

Today's decision is a victory to all Muslims who wish to preserve their identity and values despite prejudice and bigotry.

The ruling contrasts with a controversial stand by France on the same issue. Last year, France banned religious clothing and symbols in state schools, including Christian crosses and Jewish skullcaps.

Exercise Four

A plane has crashed in central Mexico, killing all 18 people on board. The DC 9 punched to the ground, shortly after taking off from Orapane, about 300 kilometers west of the capital Mexico City. The plane was on its way to the capital when it crashed. The cause of the accident is still being investigated.

Exercise Five

Insurgents carried out the single most deadly attack in Iraq since the war began. On Monday, a suicide car combing killed at least 125 people at a police recruiting center south of Baghdad. More than 150 others were injured. Iraqi officials say the violence will not derail the political development taking place in Iraq, including the formation of a new government.

Unit 13 A Different Voice

Part Two Listen Now

Text One

A small Welsh market town has put itself on the front line in the debate over joining the euro. Llangollen has declared itself a euro zone while it holds its week-long music festival. The single currency will be accepted alongside sterling during the international Eisteddfod, which attracts thousands of visitors. But as Guto Harri reports, it's not music to everyone's ears.

For half a century, and more, this Welsh hillside town has drawn dancers, singers, and musicians from all over the globe for an annual celebration of cultural diversity. 100,000 people will be here this week from more than 40 countries.

Woman 1: I'll take that off you, okay? Thank you.

European tourists have come here with their new common currency, and are delighted that most banks, shops and restaurants are taking it.

Man: It will be better for tourists.

Woman 2: If I bring euros, it saves me rushing into a bank to pick up some money.

And if the euro zone helps bring in the tourists, most local traders will be happy with it.

Woman 3: Yes, it has put Llangollen on the map. What with the effects of the foot-and-mouth and September 11th last year, hopefully things will improve and things can only get better in my view.

Text Two

This week, Californian wine workers vote on a contract proposal from winery owners. The workers have now been on strike for six weeks. The contract proposal calls for cuts in wages and cuts in benefits. The prospects for rank and file approval seem slim. A central issue of the strike is the economic well-being of the California wine industry. William Drummond reports.

A gondola containing tons of freshly picked Chardonnay grapes is dumped into a hopper as the process begins for bottling the 1986 vintage. The harvest has continued despite the fact that more than two thousand winery workers have struck in twelve of the biggest wineries in Northern and Central California. Relying on automated plants and non-union labor, members of the Winery Owners' Association have succeeded in carrying on what looks like business is usual. But out on picket line, union worker Pat Scoley is anything but pleased.

"I guess they're doing all right. If they aren't, they want us to think they are. I hope to hell they aren't, between you and me."

Part Four Here's More

Exercise One

Town Crier: Oh yea, oh, yeah, oh yea. It is no to the euro today.

Guto Harri: Anti-euro campaigners suspect this experiment has less to do with pleasing the tourists, than prompting an unpopular political project, ditching the pound.

Stuart Davies: For somebody to come along and say this is going to happen to your town, before they've, they have consulted with us. I'm afraid it makes me very angry and even more, more certain to, to, to fight against it.

Guto Harri: This essentially cultural event would not have attracted the support of the Foreign Office, Treasury, and European Commission unless there was, at the very least, a subtle political agenda. What critics of the government suspect, once again, is that the aim is to make the euro look as normal as possible, so that British entry in the end seems inevitable. Guto Harri, BBC news, Llangollen.

Exercise Two

The Union contract expired at the end of July, which is the beginning of the harvest, the time when wine makers usually need all the help they can get. But many plants are like the Charles Kruge Winery, which has been completely automated. Owner Peter Mondaby says the strike has no effect on producing the product.

"We feel that we can go on indefinitely, because there're a lot of people who want to work. And it's only a question of training these people and, of course, with the system that we have, very well computerized, that they can fit in with a reasonable amount of training, that they can fit in. So, I mean, we're not concerned about it."

Exercise Three

Wages for workers in the winery industry range from around eight dollars to fifteen dollars an hour. The union was willing to give up a slight reduction in wages, but refused to accept cuts in the pension and health benefits. The employers reportedly want a twenty percent reduction in the wages and benefits package. Winery owners say the union has to recognize that overall costs have increased.

"Not only is your gross down; the competition has forced us to increase marketing and advertising, which is further eroding whatever margin was there."

Unit 14

Abolishing Juvenile Death Penalty

Part Two Listen Now

Text One

Opponents of capital punishment won a major victory at the US Supreme Court Tuesday. By a vote of five to four, the high court ruled that it is now unconstitutional to execute criminals who were younger than 18 when they committed their crimes.

The majority opinion striking down juvenile death sentences was written by Justice Anthony Kennedy. He noted what he called the "overwhelming weight of international opinion" that has moved against the juvenile death penalty in recent years.

Justice Kennedy also wrote that American society views juveniles as, in his words, "categorically less culpable than the average criminal" because of their lack of maturity and emotional stability.

Reaction from death penalty opponents was swift and positive.

Marsha Levick is with a group called the Juvenile Law Center in New York.

Ms. Levick: We cannot impose capital punishment on offenders who do not demonstrate the same degree of adult blameworthiness, adult culpability, mature judgment as adult offenders do.

The narrow five to four decision affects 19 states that had allowed offenders under the age of 18 to be put to death. The ruling abolishes death sentences for more than 70 murderers now on death row who committed their crimes when they were 16 or 17. The Supreme Court outlawed executions for those 15 and younger back in 1988. The United States had been among a dwindling handful of countries in recent years that still permitted juvenile executions. Other nations that have been moving to end the practice include Iran, Pakistan and Saudi Arabia.

Text Two

Richard Dieter is the executive director of the Death Penalty Information Center, a group based in Washington that opposes capital punishment.

Richard Dieter: What Justice Kennedy is saying is that if we look to serving in the military, voting, drinking, age 18 is a bright line. Surely, we should apply the same standard to those who can be executed.

Justice Sandra Day O'Connor wrote a dissenting opinion for the four-member minority. She argued that even though those under 18 may be less culpable for their crimes than adults, they should still be eligible for the death penalty depending on the severity of the offense.

The decision was not welcome news for family members who have lost loved ones to teenage murderers. Bill Green and Adolph Pena both lost children to killers who committed murder at the age of 17.

Bill Green: Well, the person who killed our son had already committed over 14 felony accounts by the time he was 17 years old.

Adolph Pena: But I'd say one thing. These 17-year-olds definitely knew what they were doing when they murdered my daughter.

The Death Penalty Information Center says 22 criminals have been executed for crimes committed when they were 16 or 17 since the Supreme Court reinstated the death penalty in 1976.

The latest ruling continues a trend on the Supreme Court in recent years to restrict the use of the death penalty. The high court banned the execution of mentally retarded criminals in 2002, calling it a violation of the US Constitution's ban on cruel and unusual punishment.

Part Four Here's More

Exercise

1. She argued that even though those under 18 may be less culpable for their crimes than adults, they should still be eligible for the death penalty depending on the severity of the offense.
2. The Death Penalty Information Center says 22 criminals have been executed for crimes committed when they were 16 or 17 since the Supreme Court reinstated the death penalty in 1976.
3. As the UK cools down this week, parts of the US are again bracing themselves for rising heat and humidity levels as the latest heatwave spreads to the eastern US states.
4. At the age of 41, Joel Osteen is a religious superstar, reaching not only the more than 40,000 registered members of his church in Houston, but millions of people around the world through his televised ministry and his best-selling book, *Your Best Life Now — Seven Steps to Living at Your Full Potential*.
5. They say the bus was apparently racing a second bus to pick up passengers waiting at the next stop, when it was hit by the train.
6. Indonesian President Susilo Bambang Yudhoyono, who is on a state visit to Australia, has extended his condolences to the families of the seven men and two women who died, and says they will be

awarded the Indonesian Medal of Honor.

7. It says people preparing food in areas with avian-flu outbreaks should wash hands frequently, and all surfaces and utensils that have been in contact with raw meat should be washed and disinfected.
8. The returned Chinese students all agree that their greatest challenge was the transition to a classroom where students ask questions, reply to questions, and state and defend points of view.
9. According to Mr. Cook, "One of the issues that the United States is confronting, the reality of the situation in Iraq, is that Iraq clearly had nothing to do with 9/11 despite the administration's best efforts to kind of ally Iraq and 9/11 during the 2004 presidential election."

Unit 15

Deep in Heat

Part Two Listen Now

Text One

As the UK cools down this week, parts of the US are again bracing themselves for rising heat and humidity levels as the latest heatwave spreads to the eastern US states. The upper Midwest region has already been gripped by the latest heatwave and many parts have recorded some of the highest temperatures in years.

As the heat is expected to slowly edge further east, the New York Mayor has already declared a state of emergency in anticipation of the extreme heat. Philadelphia is expecting its first 100°F (38°C) day in five years.

The biggest concern now is that the heat is spreading into major built-up areas. New York, Washington, and Baltimore are all expecting triple-digit temperatures before the heat subsides again on Thursday.

A severe heatwave has already swept across the US during the past month and was believed to be responsible for over 140 deaths in California alone. On Monday further weather warnings and advisories were issued for the Midwest and eastern states.

The current heatwave has given good reason for the premature concern. In Minneapolis the temperatures soared to over 100 degrees Fahrenheit (38°C) for the first time in over a decade.

In Bismarck, North Dakota, the temperature reached 44°C (112°F) on Sunday. The city also had temperatures of 100°F or higher for eight days in a row, making it the hottest stretch in 132 years, since records began.

Text Two

The southwest monsoon, which brings seasonal rains to Pakistan, India and Bangladesh between June and September, is now fully set in across the Indian subcontinent. At the weekend, the monsoon rains were causing problems in parts of both Pakistan and India.

In Pakistan, several rivers were in low flood, including the Indus. Torrential rains and strong winds had brought down power lines in Karachi, and rail services to and from the city were disrupted when floods damaged a railway bridge 48 miles (78 kilometres) away. Farmers were welcoming the rain for their paddy and sugarcane crops, but their cotton and vegetable crops would suffer in the downpours.

Meanwhile around 25,000 people were moved from low-lying areas of western India, as rivers rose above danger levels and flooded large areas. The Narmada River in the state of Gujarat was one which rose dangerously high, causing alarm in riverside villages. In neighbouring Maharashtra state water levels were reportedly receding, but thousands were still moved to safer ground.

Northern India also saw weather-related problems at the weekend. Around 19 people were killed here, either due to flooding or lightning strikes, bringing the total of monsoon-related deaths in India to 343 since the monsoon set in.

Part Four Here's More

Exercise One

On 15 Aug 1952 , over 228 mm (9 in) of rain fell in a few hours, flooding the North Devon town of Camelford, Lynmouth. The floods triggered by the rain caused 34 deaths and destroyed the town.

Exercise Two

From 31 Jan to 1 Feb 1953, East Coast storms flooded low-lying parts of East Anglia. Over 300 people were killed and thousands were made homeless. Over 1,800 lives were lost in continental Europe, mainly the Netherlands. High tides had clashed with a storm surge to drive the water over the top of sea defences along the East Coast.

Exercise Three

Winter 1962–3 is the coldest recorded winter since at least 1795. On 6–7 Feb snow fell continuously for 36 hours. The average temperature during the winter was only 0.8 °C (33.4 °F). Economic activity dropped by about 7 per cent and unemployment increased with 160,000 workers being laid off. At least 49 people were killed by the direct effects of the severe weather.

Exercise Four

The Atlantic hurricane season has so far started on a rather quiet note with just three named tropical storms forming in the area since the season began on 1st June, the latest of which is tropical storm Chris.

Chris formed on Tuesday just east of the Leeward Islands in the Caribbean. The storm quickly gained strength from the warm waters of the Caribbean Sea and now has wind speeds up to 60 mph. The National Hurricane Centre is expecting the storm to strengthen to hurricane force (wind speeds over 74 mph) by Friday and therefore become the first hurricane of the 2006 season.

Chris is moving in a west-northwesterly direction and is expected to edge just north of Puerto Rico and Hispaniola before making landfall on the Bahamas by Sunday. Several warnings are already in place across many islands of the Caribbean.

Exercise Five

Summer 1976 saw a great drought. In southern England, no rain fell for between 35 and 42 days up to 29 August. It was the longest period without rain for 80 years. Reservoirs, already depleted by 1975 being the fifth driest year this century, dried up completely, causing severe water shortages in many parts of England and Wales. Over 1 million people were forced to collect their water from standpipes in the street. As the summer continued, elderly people suffered strokes and heart attacks brought on by the heat. This heatwave was caused by a high pressure area which got blocked over the British Isles. In Britain, the government passed the UK's first ever Drought Bill, creating the post of Minister for Drought. This bill gave wide powers to local authorities, allowing them to fine people for wasting water. The farming industry lost crops with an estimated value of £500 million and thousands of acres of forest were lost to fire.

Unit 16 Accidents and Catastrophes

Part Two Listen Now

Text One

At least 30 people are dead and many others injured after a passenger train slammed into a crowded bus in Sri Lanka.

Police say the accident happened about 60 kilometers northeast of the capital, Colombo on Wednesday morning.

They say the bus was apparently racing a second bus to pick up passengers waiting at the next stop, when it was hit by the train.

Witnesses say the bus driver ignored warning signals and swerved around a gate, partially blocking the railway crossing.

The packed bus burst into flames after the train crushed it and then dragged it almost 300 meters.

Police Spokesman Rienzie Perera says an investigation is under way, but it appears the train had no way to avoid the collision.

"This is due to the negligence of the driver. It was racing another bus while the gates were closed."

Officials say all of the victims were on the bus and that many of the injured are in a serious condition.

Sri Lankan troops are helping with the rescue effort.

The train was traveling to the temple city of Kandy, while the bus was on its way to the capital.

Sri Lanka has seen a number of collisions caused by buses trying to dash across railway lines. But this is one of the worst death tolls involving a train in Sri Lanka's history.

Text Two

Almost a week after a devastating eight-point-seven magnitude earthquake struck northwestern

Indonesia, aid workers are still struggling to get help to those in need. Efforts have been hampered by aftershocks, bad weather and the crash of an Australian military helicopter that left nine dead.

About 1,300 people are estimated to have died when their houses were reduced to rubble by the huge earthquake that struck off the Indonesian coast last Monday. There is now little hope of finding more survivors under the collapsed buildings, but tens of thousands of other victims are still desperately in need of assistance.

Many are living outside. Even those whose houses are still standing are too frightened to move back because of continuing aftershocks. The United States Geological Survey has registered at least 150 aftershocks, more than 20 a day.

Paul Dillon of the International Organization of Migration recently returned from the island of Nias, close to the quake's epicenter, and he says people are camping where they can.

"Obviously, these aftershocks are very traumatic for the survivors. Much of the population is living outdoors. They may be living on their verandas, in some cases outside of the city, where the traffic is very light because of the damage to the roads. Entire villages are literally living in the midst of the largest streets in the town."

Aid is getting through, however. The US Navy hospital ship Mercy, due in the area Tuesday morning, will provide much-needed extra beds for the thousands of injured, who currently need to be flown hundreds of kilometers to facilities on Sumatra Island.

Ships carrying food and water are getting through to Nias and its northern neighbor Simeulue, but the shattered roads and collapsed bridges are holding up distribution.

Most transport is by helicopter, but the air bridge suffered a terrible blow Saturday, when an Australian military helicopter crashed, killing nine of its 11 crewmembers. Their bodies were being repatriated Monday, with full military honors. Australian and Indonesian troops accompanied the flag-draped coffins into the transporter aircraft.

Indonesian President Susilo Bambang Yudhoyono, who is on a state visit to Australia, has extended his condolences to the families of the seven men and two women who died, and says they will be awarded the Indonesian Medal of Honor.

Part Four Here's More

Exercise One

More than 80 people are now known to have died in an earthquake that struck eastern Turkey early yesterday morning and almost 400 have been injured. Because of the remoteness of the region and the damaged phone lines, casualty figures are all approximate, but a Turkish government minister said he feared that the numbered killed would rise to at least 150. A school dormitory where more than 100 children were sleeping was demolished, trapping many of them inside. The earthquake, measuring 6.4 on the Richter scale struck the Turkish province of Tunceli the early hours.

Exercise Two

A cyclone with winds up to 200 kilometers an hour battered coastal towns in western India late Monday, leaving an estimated 200 persons dead. Thousands of homes were destroyed and power lines were downed in Gujarat State. A search continues for hundreds of persons aboard fishing boats off the western coast of India. The India Navy has sent a ship to rescue 350 people aboard an oil drilling barge near Bombay. The storm apparently pushed the barge away from the coast. A 500-ton oil tanker sank in Bombay harbor. And at least five members of its crew are still missing. Authorities in Gujarat State say the Air Force will drop food bundles over villages isolated by that storm.

Unit 17

Big Churches, Big Crowds

Part Two Listen Now

Text One

There is plenty of spirit in the spirituality at the Lakewood Church. Services here sometimes resemble a rock concert or theatrical event. The music is provided by a 10-piece orchestra and an onstage choir, with church-goers joining in, reading the lyrics from overhead television screens. Close-up images of Pastor Joel Osteen and others are provided by cameras on cranes and platforms placed in and around the congregation.

At the age of 41, Joel Osteen is a religious superstar, reaching not only the more than 40,000 registered members of his church in Houston, but millions of people around the world through his televised ministry and his best-selling book, *Your Best Life Now — Seven Steps to Living at Your Full Potential.* The book has sold over two million copies and been at the top of the New York Times best seller list.

The Lakewood Church is growing so fast that its present building is no longer adequate, so in July, the congregation will move to the former Compaq Center sports arena, near downtown Houston. Joel Osteen, who is overseeing the remodeling of the huge building says this will help draw even more people to his weekly services.

"It will hold 16,000 people, where our church we are in now holds eight; plus it is on the major freeway here in town, and we are more centrally located," he says. "It is just a dream come true to come out from where we are to this place, so we are excited about it."

Text Two

Critics of the Osteen approach to Christianity note that the millions of dollars being invested in the new venue could have been directed to charity. There are also some traditional Christian leaders who object to the whole megachurch trend, describing it as "watered-down Christianity."

But Rice University sociologist and religion expert William Martin says there is no question that the high-energy entertainment of the big churches is growing in popularity.

"Often these large buildings look more like civic auditoriums than they do like sanctuaries, typical sanctuaries. Some people are put off by that, others are very much attracted by it," he said. "I think you would have to say the balance is on the attracting side; these are the churches that are growing and attracting thousands and even tens of thousands of people."

Professor Martin also notes that part of Lakewood's success has to do with its openness to people from all races, ethnic groups and walks of life.

"One of the remarkable things and attractive things about the Lakewood Church, I think, is its diversity. You have 25,000 people (who attend services each week) and it is approximately a third, a third, a third — black, Hispanic, and white — with some Asians in there as well, a growing number."

Joel Osteen says he believes people from all different backgrounds are drawn to his message. "I think when you have a message to help people and you are sincere, it does not matter what color or what social status you are," he said.

Part Four Here's More

Exercise One

It's a seemingly endless stream of people, as the faithful file passed the body of Pope John Paul the second. Outside is a sea of humanity, stretching more than a mile down the road that leads to the Vatican.

They wait, sometimes for more than eight hours, often breaking into song, or shouting the pope's name and applauding. According to the Vatican, 18,000 people pass through the doors of Saint Peter's every hour. The crowds have been calm, but they keep coming, and their sheer numbers have already presented logistical problems for the city of Rome.

"Well, the biggest problem we have is transport, because people are coming and going and we have to get them to the Vatican."

But Friday's funeral will present an even bigger challenge, how to protect the more than two-million mourners and 200 dignitaries?

The problem is there are so many people in such a small area that basically time and distance are your best friends at these kinds of events.

Not surprisingly, the Vatican, a sovereign nation, has its own security force, starting with the Swiss guards. They may look like they are in place just for show, but the 100-strong military force is sworn to defend the pope to the death ... and, in the past, they have. There is another 200-person security detail, comprised of bodyguards, and a special corps from the Italian police ... Vatican security doesn't stop there.

Exercise Two

As firework displays ushered in the euro from Paris to Athens, Rome to Madrid, curiosity drove Europeans to cash machines at midnight December 31, 2001 for the first look at the brightly colored new notes. More than 300 million Europeans began changing their old currencies for the euro in the most ambitious currency changeover in history. To prepare for the large demand, banks across the euro zone disabled 200,000 ATMs in the afternoon, changing software and loading them with euro notes. Altogether 15 billion banknotes and 52 billion coins — worth 646 billion euros, or $568 billion — have been produced for the switchover.

Knowing how people can be attached to their national currencies, architects of the euro expressed hope that it will help realize dreams of a united Europe.

Across the continent, officials welcomed the euro as a sign of economic stability — a new symbol to bind 12 nations on a continent at the heart of two world wars.

"We will become a greater Europe with the euro," EU Commission President said in Vienna, shortly after he used the new currency to buy flowers for his wife. "We shall become stronger, wealthier."

His view was shared by Helmut Kohl, the former German Chancellor, who with the late French leader Francois Mitterrand had championed the single currency to bring peace and security to Europe. Kohl wrote in a newspaper, "A vision is becoming a reality. For me, the common currency in Europe fulfills a dream. It means there is no turning back from the path toward unification of our continent."

Unit 18

Golden Globe Awards

Part Two Listen Now

Text One

The Golden Globe Awards have recognized the films *The Aviator* and *Sideways* at their annual Hollywood ceremony Sunday.

These Hollywood Foreign Press Association awards are often seen as a good indicator of who will win the more prestigious Oscars next month.

The Aviator, the story of the eccentric billionaire, flight pioneer Howard Hughes, was named Best Motion Picture-Drama. And Leonardo DiCaprio was named Best Dramatic Actor for his portrayal of Hughes.

Herein this movie clip:

Hughes: I am supposed to be many things which are not complimentary. I am supposed to be capricious. I have been called a playboy. I have even been called an eccentric, but I do not believe that I have the reputation of being a liar.

Actor DiCaprio thanked director Martin Scorsese, who brought the story to the screen.

Mr. DiCaprio: Growing up in this business and truly wanting to be a part of the world of film, I'm a truly privileged person standing here today. But I must say the pinnacle of all that has been to work alongside one of the greatest contributors to the world of cinema of our time, and that is the great Martin Scorsese.

Sideways, the tale of a trip by two friends through California's wine-growing region, was named Best Musical or Comedy.

Clint Eastwood was named Best Director for *Million Dollar Baby*, the tale of a woman boxer and a veteran trainer. Along with directing the film, Eastwood played the trainer, and thanked the other stars.

Mr. Eastwood: I'd like to thank the great Hilary Swank and the world's greatest actor, Morgan Freeman.

Hilary Swank was named Best Dramatic Actress for her starring role in the film.

III. Listen and choose the best answer to each question you hear.

1. When and where was the Golden Globe Awards held?
2. How many awards did *The Aviator* win?

3. Whom was Mr. DiCaprio grateful to?
4. What award did *Sideways* win?
5. Which movie is a tale of a woman boxer and a veteran trainer?

Text Two

Jamie Foxx was named Best Actor in a Musical or Comedy for his leading role in *Ray*, a film biography of Rhythm and Blues great, Ray Charles.

Actor Foxx turned his thoughts to the late singer, who helped him prepare for the role before he died last year at age 73.

Foxx: I'm going to thank Ray Charles. I sat with Ray Charles, and I was sitting and I was playing with him. And I hit the wrong note and he said, why the hell would you do that? And I said, I don't know. He said the notes are right underneath your fingers. He said life is notes right underneath our fingers. All you've got to do is take the time to play the right notes. Ray, we are playing beautiful music right now today.

Natalie Portman and Clive Owen were both honored for their supporting roles in *Closer*, a film about two couples who learn the consequences of infidelity. Veteran filmmaker Mike Nichols directed the film.

Comedian Will Ferrell presented the award for Best Actress in a Musical or Comedy.

Will Ferrell: And the Golden Globe goes to Annette Bening.

In *Being Julia*, Annette Bening plays an egotistical actress who has an affair with a younger man in 1930s London.

The Golden Globe for Best Foreign Language Film went to *The Sea Inside* from Spain, starring Javier Bardem. It is based on a true story of a seaman who becomes quadriplegic and fights for 30 years for the right to die.

Robin Williams received a Lifetime Achievement Award, and he thanked the Hollywood Foreign Press in a half-dozen languages.

Mr. Williams: Grazie, gracias, danke, merci, spasibo, xie xie, arigato gozaimas, thank you Hollywood Foreign Press.

Part Four Here's More

Exercise One

The non-fiction book selected was Robert Caro's *Master of the Senate: The Years of Lyndon Johnson* — the third book in his lengthy biographical series on the former US president.

The author's publisher, Sonny Metha, read the message.

"I'm really lucky to be following the career and trying to untangle and understand the manipulations and devices by which Lyndon Johnson acquired and used, for good and for ill, political power."

The Fiction Award went to Julia Glass for her first published novel, *Three Junes*. Set during three summers, the book explores love in the lives of a Scottish family that makes peace with its past, and embraces its future.

Ms. Glass noted the power of books to transport readers anywhere.

"Books are like these amazing objects that are just very homely but transmute themselves into something completely different when you read them — a book can be a sailing vessel, a magic rabbit hole, a tree house, a fabulous rich dessert, the wise, crusty grandmother you lost when you were too young to need her to be around you."

Ruth Stone received the poetry prize for her eighth book, *In the Next Galaxy*, in which she writes from her vantage point as a woman in her eighties, revealing a passion for knowing how the world works.

Nancy Farmer's *The House of the Scorpion*, a futuristic story about a clone struggling to understand his existence, took home the Young People's Literature Award.

Exercise Two

1. Stunt men are those who perform stunts, especially instead of an actor in a film or television program.
2. Playwrights create scripts and tell stories through the words and actions of characters.
3. A script holder keeps a detailed record of progress when shooting a film or TV drama.
4. A producer is involved throughout all phases of motion picture production from inception to completion, including coordination, supervision and control of all other talents and crafts.
5. A director has the challenging task of bringing together the many complex pieces of a production — the script, actors, set, costuming, lighting and sound and music — into a unified whole.
6. Film editors take the raw footage shot on a movie set and select which shots, angles, performances and more to use, and then cut them together to form a cohesive and interesting story.

Unit 19

Cutting Back on Smoking in Movies

Part Two Listen Now

Text One

Dr. Jonathan Fielding, the public health director for Los Angeles County, says 80 percent of the live-action movies favored by young people portray smoking, and that the images make young viewers more likely to take up the habit.

He says the entertainment industry has done a remarkable job in helping with public health issues like AIDS, breast cancer, and hunger.

Jonathan Fielding: That is why it's so perplexing to us in public health that an industry with such a huge heart continues to ignore a proactive solution that could save tens of thousands of lives every year in the United States, and millions more worldwide.

Dr. Fielding spoke with reporters as a mobile billboard started touring Hollywood, with a message urging that smoking be kept out of youth-rated movies. The so-called International Day of Action was held February 22, in advance of the biggest day of the year in the US movie calendar, Oscar Sunday. That is the day when Hollywood turns out in all its glamour for the annual Academy Awards presentation.

Stan Glantz, a professor of medicine at the University of California, San Francisco, was one of the people behind the US movement to eliminate smoking in public places. And as city after city started imposing restrictions on smoking, he turned his attention to movies.

Stan Glantz: About 10 or 12 years ago, I started noticing that there seemed to be a lot more smoking in the movies, and started getting concerned about the problem, and after several years of going to quiet, behind-the-scenes and totally useless meetings with people in Hollywood, decided to start a public campaign to really put this issue on the public agenda.

Text Two

As part of the worldwide effort to highlight movie smoking, film screenings are being held in Senegal and Israel in which young people cough each time an on-screen actor lights a cigarette. Young people in Malaysia are meeting with reporters to discuss the smoking issue, and campaigners in India are protesting the prominent display of Marlboro cigarettes in a current Indian movie.

Professor Glantz says Hollywood sets the standard for international films, and notes that more than half of its revenues come from countries outside the United States and Canada. So his organization, called Smokefree Movies Action Network, has helped organize protests and educational events from Algeria to Vietnam and Zimbabwe.

Moviemakers, for their part, bristle at the suggestion that on-screen portrayals promote smoking, just as they question the link between movies and real-life violence or other harmful behavior. Professor Glantz says researchers have shown a conclusive tie between smoking and the movies, and adds that simple steps, such as restricting smoking to adult-only films, would address the issue without censorship.

Payments by cigarette companies for prominent placement in movies, once common in Hollywood, are no longer legal. The researcher questions, however, why so many Hollywood films show people smoking. He says regardless of the reasons, the portrayals are a form of advertising for tobacco companies.

Stan Glantz: It's advertising that people don't realize they're being advertised to. And once people are made aware of it and thinking about it, then it doesn't work for them as well any more.

He says one suggestion adopted by some theater owners in Canada could also help. Theater tickets have an anti-smoking message printed on the back. He adds that on-screen notices before a movie begins can also alert viewers to the dangers of smoking, and says such ads are now being shown in New York State and Vermont.

Mike O'Sullivan, VOA news, Los Angeles.

III. Listen and choose the best answer to each question you hear.

1. Which effort is NOT mentioned in the news to highlight movie smoking?
2. Where do more than half of Hollywood's revenues come from?
3. For their part, what do moviemakers question?

Part Four Here's More

Exercise

The Academy Awards is the main national film award in the United States of America. Its story dates back to 1927, when the Academy of Motion Picture Arts and Sciences was founded. In May 1928, the plans for an awards ceremony presented by the Awards committee were accepted. A year later, the first Academy Awards ceremony was held on May 16 in the Blossom Room of Hollywood Roosevelt Hotel. It was attended by 250 people and tickets were sold for $10 each. But today, no tickets are available for public sale; attendance is strictly by invitation only.

For most of the world, the Academy Awards is known as Oscar. It is not clear how it received such a nickname. A popular story has been that Margaret Herrick, an Academy librarian mentioned to her colleagues in 1931 that the statuette resembled her Uncle Oscar. So the Academy staff started to call it Oscar. Although the journalists used the nickname frequently during the late 1930's, officially it has been used since 1939.

Each Oscar statuette is manufactured in Chicago and depicts a knight, holding a sword, standing on a reel of film. The five spokes of the film reel signify the five original branches of the Academy: actors, directors, producers, technicians and writers.

There are also many interesting things in the history of the Academy Awards. *Titanic* and *Ben-Hur* won eleven Oscars and hold the record of winning the most Oscars. Among actors, Katherine Hepburn holds the record of most nominations and the most wins. She was nominated twelve times and gained the Oscar four times. Jack Nicholson has won three awards from his eleven nominations. In terms of big losses, Woody Allen is the record-holder. He was nominated seventeen times in all the major categories between 1927 and 1999, but he has won only three Oscars.

II. Listen and choose the best answer to each question you hear.

1. When was the first Academy Awards ceremony held?
2. How many people attended the first Academy Awards?
3. When did the nickname — Oscar — officially start to be used?
4. Where is the Oscar statuette made?
5. Which movie won the most Oscars?
6. Among actors, who holds the record of most nominations and the most wins?

Unit 20

African-American Immigrants

Part Two Listen Now

Text One

Millions of people in the United States can trace their roots back to Africa, but there is an increasing number of people who have come here directly from an African nation. These Africans in America are trying to establish their own identity and play a larger role in their communities.

When African officials and oil industry executives come to Houston, one of the places they can go to get a taste of home is Kenny's restaurant in the southwest part of the city. Owner Kenny Adebiyi, an immigrant from Nigeria, says he is also trying to build an identity for African food and culture among both black and white people living in Houston.

Kenny Adebiyi: Definitely, we are not being recognized because other cultures, like the Chinese, you know, cling to certain areas. We need that here. And that's why we are doing this, that we need to be recognized and have a place of our own.

Kenny Adebiyi and several other African immigrants have now formed a group called the African Coalition to promote the image of African immigrants in Houston and to develop some clout both politically and socially.

His friend and fellow Nigerian immigrant Sam Uzoh is especially keen on the idea of bringing a better understanding of Africa and Africans to the people of the United States. In the two stores he owns in the Houston area, Sam sells African art, crafts and clothes mostly to African Americans who want to get closer to their cultural origins. But Sam Uzoh was distressed by the questions some of them asked him.

"Isn't there something good going on in Africa? Is there anything good at all, you know, that we can see? Is just everything war and starvation and stuff like that?"

III. Listen and choose the best answer to each question you hear.

1. Where is Kenny Adebiyi's restaurant?
2. According to Kenny, why is the Chinese culture recognized in the US?
3. What is the name of the group formed by Kenny and other African immigrants?
4. Generally, who are the customers of Sam's stores?

Text Two

To counter the image created by news reports out of Africa depicting violence and poverty, Sam Uzoh began importing African movies on video tape and in the DVD format to sell in his stores.

He says this venture has been quite successful and that many customers come back for more.

Sam Uzoh: The movies have some wonderful stories, with great acting, and we go out and we pick out those movies in English and the subject matter is such that it would be of interest to Americans.

Most of the movies currently come from Nigeria, which has an active film production industry, but Sam Uzoh is on the lookout for films from elsewhere with good, compelling stories that will both entertain and educate his customers.

African immigration to the United States is small compared to immigration from many other nations. In 2003, for example, 115,000 Mexicans were admitted legally into the country, while 48,738 people from all of Africa entered.

Census data indicate there are around 27,000 African-born immigrants living in the Houston area, but members of the Houston African Coalition believe the actual number is much higher. Many Africans come here for jobs in the oil and gas industry or to study in local universities. Nigeria is by far the country that has supplied the most immigrants to the area, followed by South Africa, Egypt, Ghana and Ethiopia.

Greg Flakus, VOA news, Houston.

Part Four Here's More

Exercise

Unlike other immigrants, most Africans came to North America against their will. They were brought to America as slaves ever since the early 1600's. In 1619, the first cargo of African Americans appeared for sale in Virginia. However, this kind of trade didn't boom until the appearance of the plantation system toward the end of the seventeenth century.

After then, the enslaved Africans could be found in all parts of the country and put their hands to virtually every type of labor in North America. They tended the wheat fields and fruit orchards of New York and New Jersey; they traveled underground to mine iron and lead in the Ohio Valley; they worked the docks in New England; they operated printing press in New York City and managed households from Florida to Maine.

Although contributing a lot to this land, the African Americans were treated unfairly and brutally. By 1740, the slavery system in colonial America was fully developed. Most African Americans had no authority to make decisions about their own lives and could be bought, sold, tortured, rewarded, educated, or killed at a slaveholder's will.

In spite of this, for centuries, the African Americans had never stopped battling for freedom, for dignity, and for full participation in American society. And their efforts finally totally transformed the nation, and shaped the world we live in today.

Now, more than 35 million Americans claim African ancestry, and the number of African immigrants to the US increases every year. The story of African immigration is a long one, but its newest chapters are still being written today.

Appendix II
Answer Key

Unit 1
Childcare

Part One Before You Listen

II. Text One d Text Two c

Part Two Listen Now

Text One

III. 1. b 2. b 3. c

IV. 1. outside the home 2. grandparents 3. supervise
4. with the family 5. foreign 6. own homes

Text Two

III. 1. T 2. F 3. F 4. T 5. T

IV. 1. thirty-seven million
2. twelve and seven-tenths
3. six dollars and seventy-five cents
4. seven dollars and eighteen cents
5. nine dollars and four cents

Part Four Here's More

Exercise One

1. ten percent
2. one hundred ninety-one thousand
3. eight and one-half percent

4. sixty-one percent
5. sixty-five
6. Six percent; Thirty-eight percent; fifty-six percent

Exercise Two

1. a　　2. c　　3. b　　4. b　　5. c

Unit 2

Rags and Riches

Part One　Before You Listen

II. Text One　a, d　　Text Two　d

Part Two　Listen Now

Text One

III.
1. higher earnings
2. increase spending
3. Two hundred million
4. two hundred twenty-five thousand million
5. near their home country
6. brain drain

IV. 1. a　　2. c　　3. a

Text Two

III.
1. General Motors
2. Announced; lower its costs
3. This week
4. a) reduce; North America; thirty thousand
   b) close; twelve

IV. a, c, d, f, g, h

Part Four　Here's More

Exercise One

1. b　　2. a, b　　3. a

Exercise Two

1. T　　2. F　　3. T

Exercise Three

1. d　　2. b

Unit 3 Health

Part One Before You Listen

II. Text One b Text Two c

Part Two Listen Now

Text One

III. 1. F 2. T 3. F 4. F 5. T

IV. 1. very small, sharp needles; targeted points
2. the brain; pain; unexplained worry; sadness; disorders
3. flow of blood; amount of oxygen
4. chemical changes; pain; fight feelings of sadness

Text Two

III. 1. an amino acid found in black, green, oolong and pekoe tea
2. part of the body's defenses
3. substances that help the body react to infection
4. a substance that fights infection
5. dried coffee mixed with hot water

IV. 1. They say drinking tea may help strengthen the body's defense system against infection.
2. They first mixed some gamma delta T cells with antigens.
3. Twenty-one.
4. The tea drinkers produced five times more interferon while the coffee drinkers did not produce interferon.
5. Heart disease and cancer.

Part Four Here's More

Exercise

1. fatty substance; cells; hormones; liver
2. higher in fat and sugar; fighting fat
3. bacteria in the lungs
4. body waste; body fluids; attacks the liver
5. a blood clot; thickens and blocks the flow
6. gives pleasure to smokers; a poison; taken in large amounts

7. emergency medical methods; medical care
8. control sugar in the blood
9. drugs; treat depression
10. a natural substance; normal growth; maintenance

Unit 4 Sharks

Part One Before You Listen

II. Text One b Text Two a

Part Two Listen Now

Text One

III. 1. d 2. c 3. d 4. b

IV. 1. dinosaurs; more than two hundred million; more than three hundred fifty; less than 20 centimeters; the biggest whale shark; bones; cartilage
2. sense of smell; blood; chemicals; electrical and magnetic; nerves and muscles
3. plants in the ocean; unusual things; metal protective clothing

Text Two

III. 1. Because it helps find a way to fight human disease.
2. They eat injured and diseased fish.
3. Sharp teeth, aggressive actions and fame as fierce hunters.
4. In an American coastal town.

IV. 1. T 2. F 3. T 4. F 5. T

Part Four Here's More

Exercise

I. 1. Location and feature of the land in the tundra
2. Winter in the tundra
3. Summer in the tundra
4. Plants growing in the tundra
5. Animals living in the tundra

II. 2, 4, 6, 8

Unit 5

History of Jazz

Part One Before You Listen

II. Text One b　　Text Two b

Part Two Listen Now

Text One

III. 1. b　2. d　3. b　4. a　5. b

IV. 1. blues (music)　2. sad songs　3. 1890's　4. classic, traditional
5. the early 1900's　6. perform　7. written music　8. helped spread

Text Two

III. 1. T　2. T　3. T　4. F　5. F　6. T

IV. 1. the Golden Age　2. great performers　3. The King of Swing
4. play with orchestras　5. black and white　6. introduced

Part Four Here's More

Exercise One

I. 1. more than 2,700 years ago　2. in 776 B.C.　3. since 776 B.C.
4. in the year 397　5. 1896

II. 1. More than 2,700 years ago, the Olympics began.
2. In 776 B.C., the first recoded Olympics were held.
3. Since 776 B.C., the games had been held regularly for about 1,200 years.
4. In 397, the games were prohibited by the Roman Emperor.
5. In 1896, the first modern Olympics were held.

Exercise Two

2, 5, 4, 1, 6, 3

Unit 6

Thanksgiving Holiday

Part One Before You Listen

II. Text One a, c　　Text Two b, c

Part Two Listen Now

Text One

III. 1. On the fourth Thursday of November.
2. It's purely American.
3. A large dinner.
4. About thirty people.
5. A Muslim holiday.
6. Three.

IV. 1. T 2. F 3. F 4. T 5. F 6. F 7. T

Text Two

III. 1. b 2. a 3. c 4. b 5. b

IV. 1. potatoes; cooked; pumpkin
2. vegetarian
3. college; football; national; new; tradition
4. parades; organized; stores

Part Four Here's More

Exercise

1. Governor
2. the first female chancellor
3. a place
4. a listener (from Vietnam)
5. an island
6. a painting
7. a local radio station
8. a football club
9. a storm
10. a singer; a record company
11. the author; a top executive; a fast food company
12. a singer; a song
13. a play; the writer of the play; a holiday

Unit 7 Studying Abroad

Part One Before You Listen

II. Text One c Text Two a

Part Two Listen Now

Text One

III. 1. b 2. d 3. c

IV. 1. T 2. F 3. F 4. T

Text Two

III. 1. They are assistantships, grants, scholarships and fellowships.
2. The student helps a professor by teaching classes, grading papers and tests, or doing research in a laboratory.
3. Grants do not have to be re-paid while loans have to.
4. A scholarship is financial aid to undergraduate students; a fellowship is the same kind of aid for graduate students.
5. Students must complete forms found on the university's Web site.

IV. 1. a job a student does; receives money; attends classes for free
2. a gift of money to pay for some or all of the costs of college; private groups or organizations
3. financial aids; special abilities; athletic skills
4. the Global Tiger Scholarship; Grant-in-Aid Program

Part Four Here's More

Exercise

1. Large, varied and innovative.
2. Seven.
3. It was originally founded by religious congregations.
4. They have become comprehensive universities.
5. Two.
6. Creative thinking and presentation skills.

Unit 8 Bird Flu

Part One Before You Listen

II. Text One b, c Text Two d

Part Two Listen Now

Text One

III. 1. F 2. T 3. F 4. T

IV. 1. Because there is no evidence of anyone becoming infected with avian flu as a result of eating properly cooked meat and egg from poultry.

2. Because thorough cooking will kill any virus, including the deadly H5N1 strain of avian flu.
3. No, they run no risk of getting the virus.
4. They should ideally wear protection of their face and hands, and keep the working area hygienic.

Text Two

III. 1. A Russian village, several hundred kilometers south of Moscow

2. Sudden deaths among domesticated fowl
3. Bird flu virus carried by migratory birds
4. Imposing a quarantine around the village and destroying all fowl in the affected area
5. Extending a ban on the importation of birds and feathers from most of Russia

IV. 1. 120 2. 60 3. Thailand 4. Vietnam 5. Cambodia
6. Indonesia 7. 48 8. 90,000 9. Inner Mongolia 10. quarantine
11. seal 12. kill 13. disinfect

Part Four Here's More

Exercise

1. An acronym is a word that is formed from the first letters of several other words, while an initialism doesn't sound like a real word but just states the first letters of other words.
2. The same acronym or initialism may represent different organizations, groups or names.
3. He finds that Americans have a strong desire to reduce complete names or ideas to the shortest possible form.
4. In 1960, 12,000 acronyms could be found and now there are more than 100,000 acronyms.

Unit 9 Economy

Part One Before You Listen

II. Text One b Text Two a

Part Two　Listen Now

Text One

III. 1. F　2. F　3. T　4. F

IV. 1. deputy governor of the Reserve Bank of India; the chairman of Mitsubishi Corporation

2. problems in public infrastructure; bureaucratic delays; corruption; interstate regulations

3. entry barriers; high tariffs

Text Two

III. 1. Friday

2. Asian-African Summit

3. Jakarta

4. More than 40 heads of state from Asia and Africa

5. globalization; closer economic ties and trade; Asia; Africa

IV. 1. c　2. a　3. b

Part Four　Here's More

Exercise

1. United States Defense Secretary; British Prime Minister
2. American Secretary of State; Syrian President
3. President; former diplomat
4. American singer
5. Secretary General of NATO; Russian President
6. European Union's foreign policy chief; Palestinian leader
7. Israeli Prime Minister; Palestinian counterpart
8. vcteran American journalist
9. Algerian Prime Minister
10. United Nations Secretary General; special representative for Iraq

Unit 10 Massage

Part One　Before You Listen

II. Text One　c　　Text Two　b

Part Two Listen Now

Text One

III. 1. c 2. d 3. a

IV. 1. (big) believer; people are not scared of her
2. spread the cancer; educate them about cancer
3. full-time; more than; pain and anxiety; help them to relax

Text Two

III. 1. Its advanced cancer treatments.
2. "Alternative" implies the therapy can be used instead of conventional ones, which is not the case.
3. They always take notes of what patients say.
4. To study and test other ancient therapies.

IV. 1. F 2. F 3. T 4. T 5. F

Part Four Here's More

Exercise One

1. avian influenza/bird flu
2. Parkinson's disease
3. lung cancer
4. SARS

Exercise Two

1. an infectious illness which is like a very bad cold, but which causes a fever
2. the condition of being too fat in a way that is dangerous to health
3. the condition of not being able to sleep over a period of time
4. a disease in which the body cannot control the level of sugar in the blood
5. a serious disease caused by a virus which destroys the body's natural protection from infection, and which usually causes death
6. a serious medical condition in which the heart does not get enough blood, causing great pain and often leading to death
7. a serious disease which is infectious and can attack many parts of a person's body, especially their lungs

Unit 11 Sports Events

Part One Before You Listen

II. Text One a Text Two d

Part Two Listen Now

Text One

III. 1. c 2. b 3. a 4. b

IV. 1. 80 countries and territories; American pop music

2. fair play; mutual understanding; respect; refusing doping

3. 57 meters; 16; 84; 15

4. Italian police; no-fly zone; fighter jets

Text Two

III. 1. F 2. F 3. F 4. T 5. T

IV. 1. Germany played against Italy with intensity and the match was scoreless.

2. Italy struck twice in the closing moments of extra time.

3. Because they controlled the match and they also played against the German supporters.

4. Because it was a young team and it had not been expected to even reach the quarterfinals at this World Cup.

Part Four Here's More

Exercise

1. French football administrators
2. 1930
3. 12 years
4. Europe
5. the Americas
6. United States
7. North Korea
8. the 1980s
9. Argentina
10. 3.7 billion
11. 1.3 billion
12. 2.7 million
13. 64
14. Korea and Japan

Unit 12 Around the World

Part One Before You Listen

II. Text One a, b, c Text Two a, c, d

Part Two Listen Now

Text One

III. 1. d 2. b 3. c

IV. 1. attacks 2. Iraq 3. Tuesday
4. mortar 5. mad cow disease 6. Canada

Text Two

III. 1. F 2. T 3. F 4. F 5. T 6. T

IV. 1. 40 years 2. rains
3. Nine people 4. Monday
5. Two

Part Four Here's More

Exercise One

1. Spanish authorities 2. uncovered
3. attack 4. New York

Exercise Two

1. A fatal shooting. 2. Baghdad.
3. Tuesday. 4. A judge and his son.

Exercise Three

1. teenage Muslim 2. wear; dress
3. British 4. Wednesday.

Exercise Four

1. T 2. F 3. T

Exercise Five

1. car bombing 2. Monday 3. 125
4. 150 5. recruiting 6. south

Unit 13 A Different Voice

Part One Before You Listen

II. Text One b, c Text Two b

Part Two Listen Now

Text One

III. 1. F 2. T 3. T 4. F

IV. 1. week-long 2. half a century 3. annual
4. 100,000 5. delighted 6. local traders

Text Two

III. 1. c　2. b　3. d

IV. 1. contract　2. strike
3. benefits　4. slim
5. economic
6. more than two thousand winery workers have struck in twelve of the biggest wineries
7. anything but pleased

Part Four　Here's More

Exercise One

I. 1. b　2. b

II. 1. political project
2. the aim is to make the euro look as normal as possible, so that British entry in the end seems inevitable.

Exercise Two

1. T　2. F　3. T

Exercise Three

1. eight dollars to fifteen dollars an hour
2. the pension and health benefits
3. overall costs have increased

Unit 14 Abolishing Juvenile Death Penalty

Part One　Before You Listen

II. Text One　a　Text Two　b

Part Two　Listen Now

Text One

III. 1. d　2. a　3. b　4. d　5. d

IV. 1. international opinion　2. the average criminal　3. maturity
4. emotional stability　5. mature judgment

Text Two

III. 1. At the age of 18.　2. They didn't welcome the news/decision.
3. 22 juvenile criminals.　4. To restrict the use of the death penalty.

IV. 1. F 2. T 3. F 4. T 5. T

Part Four Here's More

Exercise

I. 1. that; even; though; depending
2. when; since
3. for; as
4. reaching; but; through; Your; Best; Life; Now
5. waiting; when
6. who; who
7. preparing; with; that
8. that; where
9. that; the; reality; that

II. Refer to the listening scripts.

Unit 15 Deep in Heat

Part One Before You Listen

II. Text One a Text Two a, c

Part Two Listen Now

Text One

III. 1. b 2. b 3. a 4. b

IV. 1. bracing themselves for
2. recorded
3. declared a state of emergency
4. triple-digit temperatures
5. soared
6. in a row

Text Two

III. 1. c 2. b 3. a 4. d

IV. 1. fully set in
2. in low flood
3. rose above danger levels
4. reportedly receding

Part Four Here's More

Exercise One

1. a 2. b 3. b

Exercise Two

1. 1953 2. flooded 3. storms
4. 300 5. 1,800 6. storm surge

Exercise Three

1. coldest 2. snowed 3. 0.8 ℃ 4. 49

Exercise Four

1. c 2. d 3. a

Exercise Five

1. T 2. F 3. T 4. T

Unit 16 Accidents and Catastrophes

Part One Before You Listen

II. Text One b Text Two c

Part Two Listen Now

Text One

III. 1. 60 kilometers northeast of the capital
2. The negligence of the bus driver
3. At least 30
4. The temple city
5. The capital

IV. 1. It was racing another bus to pick up passengers waiting at the next stop.
2. It burst into flames.
3. No. It appears the train had no way to avoid the collision.
4. No. All of the victims were on the bus.

Text Two

III. 1. Northwestern Indonesia 2. 8.7
3. About 1,300 4. At least 150, more than 20 a day

IV. 1. aftershocks; bad weather; the crash of an Australian military helicopter
2. the shattered roads; collapsed bridges
3. 7; 2; 11
4. the Indonesian Medal of Honor

Part Four Here's More

Exercise One

1. An earthquake

2. Early yesterday morning
3. Eastern Turkey/The Turkish province of Tunceli
4. 6.4 on the Richter scale
5. More than 80
6. Almost 400

Exercise Two

1. A cyclone
2. 200 km an hour
3. Late Monday
4. western India
5. 200
6. Thousands of homes; power lines; a 500-ton oil tanker
7. the Indian Navy has sent a ship to rescue, and the Air Force will drop food bundles

Unit 17

Big Churches, Big Crowds

Part One Before You Listen

II. Text One a, b Text Two a, c

Part Two Listen Now

Text One

III. 1. 41 2. More than 40,000
3. Over two million 4. remodeling

IV. 1. plenty of spirit
2. resemble
3. church-goers
4. in and around the congregation
5. huge, lively and dynamic

Text Two

III. 1. T 2. T 3. F 4. F 5. T

IV. 1. all races, ethnic groups and walks of life
2. 25,000; black; Hispanic; white; Asians
3. what color; what social status

Part Four Here's More

Exercise One

1. endless 2. people

3. the body of Pope John Paul the second
4. more than a mile
5. more than eight hours
6. 18,000
7. every hour
8. logistical problems

Answer to the question: Many people came to pay their last respect to the body of Pope John Paul the second.

Exercise Two

1. firework
2. the euro
3. midnight December 31, 2001
4. new notes

Answer to the question: Many Europeans came to see the new notes at midnight December 31, 2001.

Unit 18 Golden Globe Awards

Part One Before You Listen

II. Text One a, c   Text Two a

Part Two Listen Now

Text One

III. 1. a 2. b 3. b 4. c 5. c

IV. 1. one month; indicator
2. *The Aviator*; flight pioneer; portrayal; Best Dramatic Actor
3. the trainer; Best Director; starring role

Text Two

III. 1. He was a singer and died at 73.
2. Notes right underneath our fingers.
3. Best Actress in a Musical or Comedy.
4. A Lifetime Achievement Award.
5. He expressed his thanks in half a dozen languages.

IV. 1. Best Actor in a Musical or Comedy
2. Best Supporting
3. two couples
4. infidelity
5. Best Foreign Language Film
6. seaman
7. 30
8. the right to die

Part Four Here's More

Exercise One

1. Non-fiction
2. be following the career

3. political power
4. *Three Junes*
5. explores love
6. a magic rabbit hole
7. rich dessert
8. Young People's
9. Nancy Farmer
10. understand his existence

Exercise Two

1. Stunt men; perform stunts; an actor in a film or television program
2. Playwrights; scripts; the words and actions of characters
3. A script holder; shooting a film or TV drama
4. A producer; all phases of motion picture production
5. A director; a production; script, actors, set, costuming, lighting and sound and music
6. Film editors; the raw footage shot; movie set; shots, angles, performances and more

Unit 19

Cutting Back on Smoking in Movies

Part One Before You Listen

II. Text One a Text Two a

Part Two Listen Now

Text One

III. 1. a 2. d 3. c 4. d

IV. 1. public health 2. take up the habit
3. ignore the proactive solution 4. save millions of lives
5. professor of medicine 6. A public campaign

Text Two

III. 1. c 2. d 3. d

IV. 1. T 2. F 3. F 4. T

V. 1. they're being advertised to; it doesn't work for them
2. an anti-smoking message; alert viewers to the dangers of smoking

Part Four Here's More

Exercise

I. 1. a, c, d, f

II. 1. c 2. a 3. d 4. c 5. b 6. b

III. 1. public sale; invitation

2. an Academy librarian
3. holding a sword; the five original branches; directors; technicians

Unit 20
African-American Immigrants

Part One Before You Listen

II. Text One c Text Two b, d

Part Two Listen Now

Text One

III. 1. b 2. a 3. b 4. b

IV. 1. recognized; build an identity; promote the image; politically and socially
2. a better understanding of Africa and Africans; distressed

Text Two

III. 1. Violence and poverty.
2. Quite successful (and many customers come back for more).
3. 48,738.
4. Nigeria.

IV. 1. a, c, e 2. b, c

Part Four Here's More

Exercise

I. 1. a, e

II. 1. as slaves 2. 1619
3. tended the wheat fields 4. traveled underground
5. operated printing press 6. 1740
7. no authority 8. tortured
9. killed at a slaveholder's will

III. 1. For freedom, for dignity, and for full participation in American society.
2. More than 35 million.